The English Stage Company at the Royal Court Theatre

The English Stage Company was formed to bring serious writing back to the stage. The first Artistic Director, George Devine, wanted to create a vital and popular theatre. He encouraged new writing that explored subjects drawn from contemporary life as well as pursuing European plays and forgotten classics. When John Osborne's **Look Back in Anger** was first produced in 1956, it forced British Theatre into the modern age. But the Court was much more than a home for *'Angry Young Men'* illustrated by a repertoire that ranged from Brecht to Ionesco, by way of Jean Paul Sartre, Marguerite Duras, Wedekind and Beckett.

The ambition was to discover new work which was challenging, innovative and also of the highest quality, underpinned by the desire to discover a truly contemporary style of presentation. Early Court writers included Arnold Wesker, John Arden, David Storey, Ann Jellicoe, N F Simpson and Edward Bond. They were followed by a generation of writers led by David Hare and Howard Brenton, and in more recent years, celebrated house writers have included Caryl Churchill, Timberlake Wertenbaker, Robert Holman and Jim Cartwright. Many of their plays are now regarded as modern classics.

Since 1994 the Theatre Upstairs has programmed a major season of plays by writers new to the Royal Court, many of them first plays, produced in association with the *Royal National Theatre Studio* with sponsorship from *The Jerwood Foundation*. The writers included Joe Penhall, Nick Grosso, Judy Upton, Sarah Kane, Michael Wynne, Judith Johnson, James Stock and Simon Block.

Many established playwrights had their early plays produced in the Theatre Upstairs including Anne Devlin, Andrea Dunbar, Sarah Daniels, Jim Cartwright, Clare McIntyre, Winsome Pinnock, and more recently Martin Crimp and Phyllis Nagy.

Theatre Upstairs productions have regularly transferred to the Theatre Downstairs, as with Ariel Dorfman's **Death and the Maiden**, and last autumn Sebastian Barry's **The Steward of Christendom**, a co-production with *Out of Joint*, or to the West End, most recently with Kevin Elyot's **My Night With Reg** at the Criterion.

1992-1995 have been record-breaking years at the box-office with capacity houses for productions of **Faith Healer**, **Death and the Maiden**, **Six Degrees of Separation**, **King Lear**, **Oleanna**, **Hysteria**, **Cavalcaders**, **The Kitchen**, **The Queen & I**, **The Libertine**, **Simpatico**, **Mojo** and **The Steward of Christendom**.

Death and the Maiden and **Six Degrees of Separation** won the Olivier Award for Best Play in 1992 and 1993 respectively. **Hysteria** won the 1994 Olivier Award for Best Comedy, and also the Writers' Guild Award for Best West End Play. **My Night with Reg** won the 1994 Writers' Guild Award for Best Fringe Play, the Evening Standard Award for Best Comedy, and Best Comedy 1994 Olivier Awards. Jonathan Harvey won the 1994 Evening Standard Drama Award for Most Promising Playwright, for **Babies**. Sebastian Barry won the 1995 Writers' Guild Award for Best Fringe Play for **The Steward of Christendom** and also the 1995 Lloyds Private Banking Playwright of the Year Award. Jez Butterworth won the 1995 George Devine Award for Most Promising Playwright, was named New Writer of the Year for by the Writers' Guild and won the Evening Standard Award for Most Promising Newcomer 1995 for **Mojo** and the 1995 Olivier Award for Best Comedy. Phyllis Nagy won the 1995 Writers' Guild Award for Best Regional Play for **Disappeared**. Martin McDonagh won the 1996 George Devine Award for Most Promising Playwright for **The Beauty Queen of Leenane**. The Royal Court was the overall winner of the 1995 Prudential Award for the Arts for creativity, excellence, innovation and accessibility, and the 1995 Peter Brook Empty Space Award for innovation and excellence in theatre.

Now in its temporary homes The Duke Of York's and Ambassadors Theatres, during the two year long refurbishment of the its Sloane Square base, the Royal Court continues to present the best in new work. After four decades the company's aims remain consistent with those established by George Devine. The Royal Court is still a major focus in the country for the production of new work. Scores of plays first seen at the Royal Court are now part of the national and international dramatic repertoire.

The Royal Court would like to thank the following for their help with this production:

Silver Johnny photographer -Jason Bell; Set and auditorium painted by Paddy Hamilton; Specialist riggi ng by Vertico Rigging Ltd; Brickworks by Theresa Kelly; ARBITER GROUP (Fender Electronics); Original 45 and 78 lables courtesy of Trevor Churchill and John Broven at ACE RECORDS; BT MUSEUM; BRANDS HERITAGE; COURAGE BERKSHIRE BREWERY; Ken Thomas, COURAGE ARCHIVES; ALFRED DUNHILL ARCHIVE COLLECTION; Seeburg Jukebox supplied by R.G. EDWARDS AMUSEMENT MACHINES; Fablon - the sticky backed plastic - provided by FORBO CP LTD 01670 718220; cake by THE GREENWICH BREAD AND CAKE COMPANY 0181 692 0084; herbal cigarettes donated by HONEYROSE PRODUCTS LTD; JUKEBOX SERVICES 0181 943 1700; LOCKWOOD AUDIO; QUEENS THEATRE, HORNCHURCH; RONSON PLC 0171 245 6009; THEATRE ROYAL, STRATFORD EAST; Bazooka Joe's from TOPPS INTERNATIOANL LTD; UNICORN ARTS THEATRE; thanks due to Julie Cuthbert of Tolhurst Fisher (Solicitors) for advice on contracts - arranged through Business in the Arts; Wardrobe care by Persil and Comfort courtesy of Lever Brothers Ltd, refrigerators by Electrolux and Philips Major Appliances Ltd.; kettles for rehearsals by Morphy Richards; video for casting purposes by Hitachi; backstage coffee machine by West 9; furniture by Knoll International; freezer for backstage use supplied by Zanussi Ltd 'Now that's a good idea.' Hair styling by Carole at Moreno, 2 Holbein Place, Sloane Square 0171 730 0211; Closed circuit TV cameras and monitors by Mitsubishi UK Ltd. Natural spring water from Wye Spring Water, 149 Sloane Street, London SW1, tel. 0171-730 6977. Overhead projector from W.H. Smith; Sanyo U.K for the backstage microwave.

The Royal Court Theatre

presents

WITHDRAWN

MOJO

by Jez Butterworth

First performance at the Royal Court Theatre Downstairs, St Martins Lane 10 October 1996.
First performance at the Royal Court Theatre Downstairs, Sloane Square 14 July 1995.

The Royal Court presents this production by arrangement with Pola Jones Associates Ltd.

The Royal Court Theatre is financially assisted
by the Royal Borough of Kensington and Chelsea.
Recipient of a grant from the Theatre Restoration
Fund & from the Foundation for Sport & the Arts.
The Royal Court's Play Development Programme
is funded by the Audrey Skirball-Kenis Theatre.

PRUDENTIAL AWARDS
FOR THE ARTS

1995

Roy

firstcall
0171 420 0100

FUNDED BY
LONDON
BOROUGH
GRANTS
COMMITTEE

Funded by
THE
ARTS
COUNCIL
OF ENGLAND

How the Royal Court is brought to you

The Royal Court (English Stage Company Ltd) is supported financially by a wide range of public bodies and private companies, as well as its own trading activities. The company receives its principal funding from the **Arts Council of England**, which has supported the Royal Court since 1956. The **Royal Borough of Kensington & Chelsea** gives an annual grant to the Royal Court Young People's Theatre and provides some of its staff. The **London Boroughs Grants Committee** contributes to the cost of productions in the Theatre Upstairs.

Other parts of the company's activities are made possible by business sponsorships. Several of these sponsors have made a long-term commitment. 1996 saw the sixth Barclays New Stages Festival of Independent Theatre, supported throughout by **Barclays Bank**. **British Gas North Thames** supported three years of the Royal Court's Education Programme. Sponsorship by **WH Smith** helped to make the launch of the Friends of the Royal Court scheme so successful.

1993 saw the start of our association with the **Audrey Skirball-Kenis Theatre**, of Los Angeles, which is funding a Playwrights Programme at the Royal Court. Exchange visits for writers between Britain and the USA complement the greatly increased programme of readings and workshops which have fortified the company's capability to develop new plays.

In 1988 the **Olivier Building Appeal** was launched, to raise funds to begin the task of restoring, repairing and improving the Royal Court Theatre, Sloane Square. This was made possible by a large number of generous supporters and significant contributions from the **Theatres Restoration Fund**, the **Rayne Foundation**, the **Foundation for Sport and the Arts** and the **Arts Councils Incentive Funding Scheme**.

The Company earns the rest of the money it needs to operate from the Box Office, from other trading and from the transfers of plays such as **Death and the Maiden**, **Six Degrees of Separation**, **Oleanna** and **My Night With Reg** to the West End. But without public subsidy it would close immediately and its unique place in British Theatre would be lost. If you care about the future of arts in this country, please write to your MP and say so.

Autumn at the Royal Court

Theatre Downstairs
St Martins Lane WC2

From 28 Nov
The Royal Court and Druid Theatre Co. present
THE BEAUTY QUEEN OF LEENANE
by Martin McDonagh
Winner, George Devine Award 1996
for Most Promising Playwright
"An absolute cracker"
Financial Times

Theatre Upstairs
West Street WC2

Until 26 Oct - Circle
World Premiere
ASHES TO ASHES
written and directed by
Harold Pinter

26 Sept - 19 Oct - Stage
The Royal Court and Out of Jointt present
SHOPPING AND F£££ING
by Mark Ravenhill

28 Oct - 16 Nov
STORMING
The Royal Court/Marks & Spencer
Young Writers' Festival

19 Nov - 7 Dec - Stage
The Royal Court, Tamasha Theatre Co. and
Birmingham Repertory Theatre present
EAST IS EAST
by Ayub Khan Din

27 Nov - 21 Dec
I LICKED A SLAG'S DEODORANT
written and directed by
Jim Cartwright

MOJO
by Jez Butterworth

Cast *in alphabetical order*

Sweets	**Callum Dixon**
Micky	**Simon Kunz**
Silver Johnny	**Daniel Newman**
Baby	**Paul Reynolds**
Potts	**Neil Stuke**
Skinny	**Darren Tighe**

Director	*Ian Rickson*
Designer	*Ultz*
Lighting Design	*Ultz & Mark Ridler*
Sound Designer	*Paul Arditti*
Music	*Stephen Warbeck*
Production Manager	*Edwyn Wilson*
Stage Manager	*Martin Christopher*
Deputy Stage Manager	*Katy Hastings*
Assistant Stage Manager	*Debbie Green*
Assistant Director	*Rufus Norris*
Assistant Designer	*Libby Watson*
Costume Supervisor	*Jennifer Cook*
Fight Director	*Terry King*
Choreographer	*Quinney Sacks*
Voice Coach	*Joan Washington*
Production Photographer	*Ivan Kyncl*
Set Construction	*Stage Surgeons Ltd.*
	(0171 237 2765)

Jez Butterworth (writer)
Mojo is Jez Butterworth's first play, for which he received the 1995 George Devine Award for Promising Playwright, the 1995 Evening Standard Award for Most Promising Newcomer and the 1995 Olivier Award for Best Comedy.

Paul Arditti
(sound design)
For the Royal Court work includes: The Lights, The Thickness of Skin, Sweetheart, Bruises, Pale Horse, The Changing Room, Hysteria, Rat in the Skull (Royal Court Classics), The Steward of Christendom (and Out of Joint), Mojo, Simpatico, The Strip, The Knocky, Blasted, Peaches, Some Voices, Thyestes, My Night with Reg, The Kitchen, Live Like Pigs, Search and Destroy. Other theatre sound design includes: As You Like It (RSC); Tartuffe (Manchester Royal Exchange); The Threepenny Opera (Donmar Warehouse); Hamlet (Gielgud); Piaf (Piccadilly); St. Joan (Strand & Sydney Opera House); The Winter's Tale, Cymbeline, The Tempest, Antony & Cleopatra, The Trackers of Oxyrhynchus (Royal National Theatre); The Gift of the Gorgon (RSC

& Wyndhams); Orpheus Descending (Theatre Royal, Haymarket & Broadway); The Merchant of Venice (Phoenix & Broadway); A Streetcar Named Desire (Bristol Old Vic); The Winter's Tale (Manchester Royal Exchange); The Wild Duck (Phoenix); Henry IV, The Ride Down Mount Morgan (Wyndhams); Born Again, Fortune's Fool (Chichester); Three Sisters, Matador (Queens); Twelfth Night, The Rose Tattoo (Playhouse); Two Gentlemen of Verona, Becket, Cyrano de Bergerac (Theatre Royal, Haymarket); Travesties (Savoy); Four Baboons Adoring the Sun (Lincoln Center, 1992 Drama Desk Award).
Opera includes: Gawain, Arianna (ROH); The Death of Moses (Royal Albert Hall).
TV includes: The Camomile Lawn.

Callum Dixon
Theatre includes: Rosencrantz and Guildenstern Are Dead, Somewhere, The Wind in the Willows, The Recruiting Officer (RNT), Acrington Pals, Mowgli's Jungle (Octagon, Bolton); All I Want is to be an Ugly Sister (Lilian Bayliss Theatre); Waiting at the

Water's Edge (Bush); Edward II, Richard III, Two Shakespearian Actors (RSC); Macbeth (British Actors Co); Voytex (RNT Studio). Television includes: The Queen's Nose, The Tomorrow People, Odd One Out, Scene - Grey Areas, The Bill.
Film includes: Waterlands.
Radio includes: The Wolfgang Chase.

Simon Kunz
For the Royal Court: Live Like Pigs.
Other theatre includes: Barnestorming, After the Funeral, Heir of Diogenes, The Peace of Westphalia (Edinburgh Festival); Much Ado About Nothing (Holland Park Open Air Theatre); One Flew Over the Cuckoo's Nest (New Vic Touring Co.); King Lear, As You Like It (Oxford Stage Co.); Don Gil of the Green Breeches, Madness in Valencia (Gate Theatre); Richard III, (RNT); The Park (RSC).
Television includes: Between the Lines, The Bill, Pie in the Sky, Frontiers, This Life, Harry Enfield and Chums, Trip TV with Chris Morris.

Film includes: Four Weddings and a Funeral, Young Poisoners Handbook, Golden Eye.

Daniel Newman
Theatre includes: Yo-Yo by Dino Mahoney (Warehouse Theatre Co.). Television includes: Back-up, The Hello Girls, Sometime Never, A Touch of Frost, Absolutely Fabulous, The Borrowers, Men of the World, Bonjour la Class, Crown Prosecutor, The Waiting Room, Sherlock Holmes - Napoleon of Crime, The Bill, Our Tune. Film includes: The Life and Death of Phillip Knight, Jacob, Robin Hood Prince of Thieves, Dracula, The Whipping Boy, Before the Rain, Shopping, Down Amongst the Dead Men.

Ian Rickson *(director)*
For the Royal Court: The Lights, Mojo, Pale Horse, Ashes and Sand, Some Voices, Wildfire, 1992 Young Writers' Festival, Killers. Other theatre includes: The House of Yes (Gate Theatre); Me and My Friend (Chichester Festival Theatre); Queer Fish (BAC); First Strike (Soho Poly).

Opera includes: La Serva Padrona (Broomhill). Ian is an Associate Director at the Royal Court.

Mark Ridler
(co-lighting design) Mark works equally in dance, opera & theatre. Theatre designs include: Krapp's Last Tape (Bloomsbury Festival); Flying Ashes (ICA); And Our Own Kind, The Cutting (Bush Theatre); Kindertransport (Soho Theatre Co); Leave Taking (Royal National Theatre); The Lovers (Gate Theatre); Comic Cuts (Derby Playhouse & tour); Servant of Two Masters, The Wind in the Willows (Sheffield Crucible); The Tempest (World tour). Resident designer at Nottingham Playhouse 1991-1995 where lighting designs include: Macbeth, The Cherry Orchard, What the Butler Saw, Les Miserables, The Caretaker, Big Night Out. Dance includes: resident lighting designer for Leeds-based Phoenix Dance including European & British tours; Adzido Dance Company tour. Opera includes: The Rake's Progress, La Voix Humaine (Bloomsbury Festival); The Marriage of Figaro, Werther (London City Opera at Westminster

Theatre); Lost in the Stars (1991 Brighton Festival); Cosi fan tutte (ENO); 1996 Garsington Festival; La Traviata, Fidelio (Opera Northern Ireland).

Paul Reynolds
Theatre includes: Brighton Beach Memoirs (RNT, Aldwych, Gaiety Theatre Dublin and Thorndike Theatre Leatherhead); The Bed Before Yesterday (Almeida); Punk's Not Dead (Edinburgh Festival).
Television includes: Diana, Nobody's Perfect, No Place Like Home, Terry and June, Great Writers - Marcel Proust, Press Gang, All Good Things, The Bill, Exam Conditions, Casualty, Frank Stubbs Promotes, Money for Nothing, Minder, Dirty Something, Here Comes the Mirror Man, Cone Zone, The All New Alexi Sayle Show, Absolutely Fabulous, The Ghostbusters of East Finchley.
Film includes: Game of Endurance, Castaway, Slipstream, Great Expectations, Let Him Have It, The Cutter, Blue Juice.
Radio includes: King Street Juniors, The Woman Hater, Hit the Decks, Time Hops.

Neil Stuke

For the Royal Court:
Not a Game for Boys.
Other theatre includes:
The Philanderer
(Hampstead); Romeo and
Juliet, View from the
Bridge, Drinking in
America, What the Butler
Saw (Royal Exchange
Manchester); Soundings
(Old Red Lion); Grapes of
Wrath (Crucible); Woman
in Mind (Palace Watford
& USA); Goldhawk Road,
Clocks and Whistles
(Bush).
Television includes: Drop
the Dead Donkey, The
Bill, Downtown Lagos,
Rides 2, Poirot, Between
the Lines, Heartbeat, The
Chief, Cardiac Arrest,
Resort to Murder,
Karaoke, A Touch of
Frost, Thief Takers, Out
of the Blue, Game On,
Pie in the Sky.
Radio includes:
Teenage Detective.
Films include: Century,
Borderland, Suckers. Film
to be released: Shark
Hunt, Masculine
Mescaline.

Darren Tighe

For the Royal Court:
Sweetheart.
Other theatre includes:
Off Out (Hull Truck,
Edinburgh Festival and
Riverside Studio).
Television includes: Band
of Gold II, A Touch of
Frost, Dalziel and Pascoe,
Medics, Casualty, Go

Now, Cracker, Never
Mind, In Your Dreams,
No Child of Mine.
Film includes: Jude the
Obscure.

Ultz

(design & co-lighting
design)
Since designing *Mojo* last
summer at the Royal.
Court, Ultz has directed
and designed *Summer
Holiday* at Blackpool
Opera House, and
designed Handel's *Zerxes*
at Bayerische Staatsoper
in Munich.
He is currently preparing
designs for Ian Rickson's
production of *Mojo* for
Steppenwolf Theatre
Company in Chicago, for
Emil Wolk's new devised
piece at the Royal
Exchange Manchester,
and for *The Servant of
Two Masters* which he is
directing with Martin
Duncan at Nottingham
Playhouse.

Stephen Warbeck

(music)
For the Royal Court:
Harry and Me, Simpatico,
The Editing Process,
Some Voices, The
Kitchen, Blood, A Lie of
the Mind, Greenland,
Bloody Poetry, Built on
Sand, Royal Borough,
Downfall.
Other theatre music
includes: An Inspector
Calls (transferred to
Broadway & Tokyo),

Machinal, At Our Table,
The Mother, Roots,
Magic Olympical Games
(RNT); The Taming of
the Shrew, The Cherry
Orchard, The White Devil
(RSC); Damned for
Despair, Figaro Gets
Divorced, Pioneers &
Purgatory in Ingolstadt,
Canterbury Tales,
Judgement Day (Gate
Theatre).
Recent TV music
includes: Prime Suspect
(BAFTA nomination);
The Changeling,
Skallagrigg (BAFTA
nomination); You Me and
Marley; Bitter Harvest;
In the Border Country;
Roots; Nona; Happy Feet;
Bambino Mio; Meat;
Blood & Water; Devil's
Advocate; Bramwell; The
Chemistry Lesson,
Nervous Energy, Truth
or Dare.
Film scores include:
Sister My Sister; O Mary
This London; Marooned;
Crossing the Border.
Stephen has also written
music for many BBC
Radio plays, writes for
his band The hKippers,
and the Metropolitan
Water Board.

Share more fully in the life of the Royal Court Theatre... become a Patron or Benefactor

Join our supporters and invest in the future of new theatre. Call the Development Department on 0171-930-4253

Many thanks to all our supporters for their vital and on-going commitment

Stage Hands Appeal

Royal Court Theatre

The history of the Royal Court Theatre is one of survival. Harley Granville Barker during his famous 1904-7 stewardship described the building as 'frightful'. George Devine thought it 'too small, too restricted'. Successive artistic directors, artists and managers have all bemoaned the appalling conditions yet, in spite of it all, have managed to create one of the most important theatrical legends of the British theatre.

Each generation has fiddled with the Royal Court Theatre's physical bearings. The 1888 structure was modified in 1921, bombed in the blitz, rebuilt in 1952, altered in 1954, messed about with in 1964, designed but never rebuilt in 1967 and repainted with the same brown every ten years or so.

Now, in our 40th anniversary year, the Royal Court has been given a unique opportunity.

A £16.2 million award from the National Lottery, through the Arts Council of England, means that for the first, and perhaps only time, we have the chance to completely repair and restore the crumbling fabric of our building.

But there's a twist in the tale.

The Royal Court hasn't yet been given the full award, and Lottery money will only be released if we can raise partnership funding from the public: from friends and theatre-goers like you. Without your help we lose the lot.

We need to raise £500,000 from our audience members and friends towards our partnership funding target of over £5 million. Early fundraising has already raised more than £150,000, which is a great start, and you can help us to continue this success by supporting our Stage Hands appeal.

A donation of £10 towards the appeal will help get the redevelopment work started, paying for around 20 bricks. A gift of £50 will buy one square metre of reclaimed timber flooring. And a gift of £100 will help secure the theatre's foundations, paying for a cubic metre of concrete.

The Royal Court needs your help to secure the future of our theatre well into the next century.
If you'd like to know more please call Jacqueline Simons on 0171-930-4253.

THE ROYAL COURT

DIRECTION
Artistic Director
Stephen Daldry
Assistant to the
Artistic Director
Marieke Spencer
Deputy Director
James Macdonald
Associate Directors
Elyse Dodgson
Ian Rickson
Garry Hynes*
Max Stafford-Clark*
Caroline Hall *(Gerald Chapman Award)*
Trainee Director
Rufus Norris #
Casting Director
Lisa Makin
Literary Manager
Graham Whybrow
Literary Associate
Stephen Jeffreys*
Writer in Residence
David Lan*
Resident Playwright
Meredith Oakes*
(Thames Television Theatre Writers Award)
Education Co-ordinator
Amanda Stuart
International Assistant
Aurélie Mérel

PRODUCTION
Production Manager
Edwyn Wilson
Deputy Production
Manager
Paul Handley
Production Development
Manager
Simon Harper
Head of Lighting
Johanna Town
Senior Electricians
Matthew O'Connor
Alison Buchannon
Liz Poulter
Assistant Electricians
Trace Roberts-Shaw
Steve Pace
LX Board Operator
Matthew Bullock
Head of Stage
Martin Riley
Senior Carpenters
David Skelly
Christopher Shepherd
Head of Sound
Paul Arditti
Deputy Sound
Simon King
Sound Assistant
Neil Alexander
Production/IT Assistant
Mark Townsend
Head of Wardrobe
Jennifer Cook

MANAGEMENT
Executive Director
Vikki Heywood
Assistant to the
Executive Director
Josephine Campbell
Administrator
Alpha Hopkins
Administrative Assistant
Tracey Nowell
Finance Director
Donna Munday
Development Finance Officer
Neville Ayres
Finance Assistant
Rachel Harrison
Project Manager
Tony Hudson
Assistant to Project Manager
Monica McCormack

MARKETING & PRESS
Marketing Manager
Jess Cleverly
Press Manager *(0171-565-5055)*
Anne Mayer
Marketing Co-ordinator
Lisa Popham
Publicity Assistant
Peter Collins
Box Office Manager
Heidi Fisher
Deputy Box Office Manager
Terry Cooke
Box Office Sales Operators
Emma O'Neill
Laura Brook
Sophie Pridell
Ruth Collier*
Margaret McManus*

DEVELOPMENT
Development Director
Joyce Hytner
Development Manager
Jacqueline Simons
Development Co-ordinator
Sue Winter*
Special Events Co-ordinator
Lucinda Craig Harvey*

FRONT OF HOUSE
Theatre Manager
Gary Stewart
Deputy Theatre Managers
Yvette Griffith
Tim Brunsden
Duty House Manager
Rachel Fisher
Relief Duty House Manager
Anthony Corriette
Bookshop Supervisors
Del Campbell*
Catherine Seymour*
Maintenance
Greg Piggot*
Lunch Bar Caterer
Andrew Forrest*
Stage Door/Reception
Jemma Davies
Lorraine Benloss*

Charlotte Frings*
Tyrone Lucas*
Marguerite Bullard*
Andonis Anthony*
Cleaners
Maria Correia*
Mila Hamovic*
Peter Ramswell*

YOUNG PEOPLE'S THEATRE
Director
Dominic Tickell
Youth Drama Worker
Ollie Animashawun
Outreach Co-ordinator
Dominic Campbell
Special Projects
Julie-Anne Robinson
Administrator
Aoife Mannix

*= part-time

= Arts Council of England/
Calouste Gulbenkian Foundation/
Esmee Fairbairn Charitable Trust

MOJO

The Characters

MICKEY, *thirties*

BABY, *twenties*

SILVER JOHNNY, *seventeen*

SWEETS, *early twenties*

POTTS, *early twenties*

SKINNY, *early twenties*

The Setting and Time

Act One takes place upstairs at Ezra's Atlantic in Dean Street, Soho, July 1958.

Act Two takes place downstairs in the club and starts around 6 p.m. on the same day.

Act One, Scene One

Upstairs at the Atlantic. SILVER JOHNNY *stands alone. We hear the drums, the thudding bass, the screams from the club below.* SILVER JOHNNY *does steps by himself, tight, menacing, explosive, like a boxer in the seconds before a fight. A low distorted voice announces the act, the girls scream, but he keeps them waiting. The music rises, faster, louder. It reaches its height,* SILVER JOHNNY *stands at the top of the steel staircase. When the moment comes, he vaults into the stairwell and vanishes, enveloped by sound.*

The drums pound on in the blackout. Suddenly they stop and the next second we are back upstairs at the Atlantic, after the show. SWEETS *and* POTTS *are sitting at a table. There is a pot of tea on the table with three pretty cups, on a tray. The door to the back room is shut.*

SWEETS. Is that brewed?

POTTS. Four minutes.

SWEETS. You want a pill?

POTTS. My piss is black.

SWEETS. It's the white ones. Don't eat no more of the white ones. (*Pause.*) So where is he sitting?

POTTS. Who?

SWEETS. Mr. Ross.

POTTS. He's on the couch.

SWEETS. Right.

POTTS. Mr. Ross is on the couch.

SWEETS. Good. How is he?

POTTS. What?

SWEETS. Good mood, bad mood, quiet, jolly, upfront, offhand. Paint me a picture.

POTTS. Tan suit. No Tie. Penny Loafers. No tassle.

SWEETS. Uh-huh. Right. Does he look flush?

POTTS. He's Mr. Ross.

SWEETS. Absolutely.

POTTS. He's a flush man.

SWEETS. Naturally.

POTTS. Ten Guinea Baltimore loafers. Suit sweat a year for you couldn't buy. Shirt undone. Tanned like a darkie. Yes he looks flush.

SWEETS. Ten Guinea Baltimores? Fuck me briefly.

POTTS. Penny. No tassle.

SWEETS. They're *talking about it* aren't they . . . (*Pause.*) Okay. Okay. So where's Ezra?

POTTS. Ezra's at the desk, but he's not in his chair. He's round here to one side.

SWEETS. The Mr. Ross side or the miles away side?

POTTS. Round here to the side on the poochy stool.

SWEETS. Poochy stool. Good.

POTTS. Sit behind the desk it's like I'm the man. Like I'm trying to big you out. Sit round the side on the poochy stool, Hey Presto, we're all a circle.

SWEETS. Okay. Okay. So where's the kid?

POTTS. Couch.

SWEETS. Couch. Good.

POTTS. On the couch with Mr. Ross.

SWEETS. Exactly. Let him see the merchandise.

They sit there, waiting for the tea to brew.

You know Beryl? She goes to me tonight, she goes 'When Silver Johnny sings the song my pussyhair stands up.'

POTTS. Relax.

SWEETS. I know. I know. Her pussyhair.

POTTS. We just sit here.

SWEETS. I know. Her fucking minge. Her fur. *It stands up.*

POTTS. I see these girls. It's voodoo. Shaking it like they hate it. Like they hate themselves for it.

SWEETS. In the alley. 'Get it out,' she says. 'Get it out I'll play a tune on it . . . '

POTTS. One day he's asking his mum can he cross the road the next he's got grown women queueing up to suck his winkle.

SWEETS. Seventeen. Child.

POTTS. These girls. They shit when he sings.

SWEETS. Exactly. (*Beat.*) What?

POTTS. Mickey knows. They shit. He seen it.

SWEETS. They what?

POTTS. It's a sex act. It's sexual.

SWEETS. Hold it. Hold it. Stop. Wait. (*Beat.*) They *shit?*

POTTS. All over.

SWEETS (*beat*). What does that mean?

POTTS. Means they have no control in front of a shiny-suited child. Sad fucking world. The end. I'm going to use this as a rule for life: 'Anything makes polite young ladies come their cocoa in public is worth taking a look at.'

SWEETS. Good rule.

POTTS. Great rule.

SWEETS. There's got to be rules and that's a rule.

POTTS. What time is it? Okay. Good. Sweets. Listen. (*Beat.*) When he announces it –

SWEETS. Hey –

POTTS. When Ezra –

SWEETS. Hey. Hey –

POTTS. If he takes you aside . . . (I know. I know. But listen) –

SWEETS. Could be me could be you. Could be me could be you.

POTTS. Exactly. I'm planning. I'm . . . listen. He takes you aside tells you takes me aside, it's not important. For me there's no difference.

SWEETS. It's exactly the same thing. Me or you. Exactly.

POTTS. Exactly. Good. The important thing is *whichever way it comes*, when he announces it, when it *happens*, act 'Surprised and Happy'.

SWEETS. Surprised and Good. Good.

POTTS. Happy and Good. Good. The end. That's four minutes. (POTTS *stands and picks up the tea-tray.*) What?

SWEETS. Absolutely. What? Nothing.

POTTS. I'll be straight back.

SWEETS. Right. Good luck.

POTTS. Relax.

SWEETS. I am relaxed. I'm talking.

> POTTS *takes the tea into the back room. He closes the door.* SWEETS *lights a cigarette.* POTTS *returns.*

So?

POTTS. So what?

SWEETS. So what happened?

POTTS. Nothing.

SWEETS. Right.

POTTS. They're drinking the tea.

SWEETS. Right. Good. What about the Campari? Has the kid drunk his Campari?

POTTS. He's sipping it.

SWEETS. Good.

POTTS. It's casual.

SWEETS. Good sign.

POTTS. You know? Loose.

SWEETS. Excellent. Excellent sign.

POTTS. Ezra's still on the poochy stool. But he's moved it. He's tugged it over in snug next to Sam.

SWEETS. Hold it. Hold it. Stop. Who?

POTTS. What?

SWEETS. You said Sam.

POTTS. Indeed.

SWEETS. Who's Sam?

POTTS. Mr. Ross.

SWEETS. Oh.

POTTS. Sam is Mr. Ross.

SWEETS. Oh Right.

POTTS. Sam Ross. That's his name.

SWEETS. Since when?

POTTS. Everyone calls him Sam. His mum named him Sam.

SWEETS. Lah-di-dah.

POTTS. Listen. Sam Ross is here next to Ezra he's got his legs crossed and he's letting his loafer hang off his foot like this. It's bobbing there.

SWEETS. Don't.

POTTS. Right next to Ezra's leg.

SWEETS. Stop.

POTTS. Eyes wide like this. Both of 'em. Like long lost puppies.

SWEETS. Fuck me. They're talking about it aren't they.

POTTS. And remember: Sam Ross came to us.

SWEETS. He did. (*Beat.*) What's the kid doing?

POTTS. Nothing. Sitting in between looking pretty.

SWEETS. Good.

POTTS. He ain't saying nothing. Just sitting there looking foxy.

SWEETS. Good. The kid's doing good.

POTTS. He knows why he's there. He's paid to warble and look pretty. He ain't paid to give it large in the backroom.

SWEETS. Has he got the jacket on?

POTTS. Who?

SWEETS. The kid. Has he got the Silver Jacket on?

POTTS. He's took it off. It's on the table.

SWEETS. Hang on. Hang on. He's took it off?

POTTS. It's on the table.

SWEETS. Hang on. Hang on. What the fuck is he doing?

POTTS. What?

SWEETS. What the fuck is going on?

POTTS. What's up?

SWEETS. He's supposed to wear the Silver Jacket. He's Silver Johnny. Silver Johnny, Silver Jacket.

POTTS. Sweets –

SWEETS. Silver Johnny, Silver suit. That's the whole point.

POTTS. I know.

SWEETS. Ezra buys the Silver Jacket he should wear it.

POTTS. It's hot in there.

SWEETS. I don't give a fuck if it's hot. Mr. Ross deserves the full
    benefit. He's not called Shirtsleeves Johnny is he. He was called
    Shirtsleeves Johnny it would be perfect.

POTTS. It's laid back. It's a jackets off atmosphere. He's right to take
    the jacket off. It's good.

SWEETS. I'm not happy. (*Pause.*) Has he got the trousers on?

POTTS. What?

SWEETS. Has he got the silver trousers on?

POTTS. Of course he fucking has.

SWEETS. Well that's something.

POTTS. Fuck do you think they're doing in there? He's gonna sit
    there in just his pants?

SWEETS. I know. I'm just excited.

POTTS. He's got his trousers on.

SWEETS. I know. Relax.

POTTS. You relax.

SWEETS. I am relaxed. I'm talking.

POTTS. Exactly. (*Pause.*) Ezra done this. (POTTS *winks.*)

SWEETS. At you?

POTTS. Ezra don't forget. I mean who fucking discovered the kid?
    I did.

SWEETS. Right.

POTTS. Fact. One solid gold forgotten fact. Ask Mickey. Up Camden.
    Luigi's.

SWEETS. Luigi who fucks dogs.

POTTS. Yes. No. Luigi with the daughter. Parkway. With the Italian
    flag up behind the. The thing behind the.

SWEETS. With the daughter. Does the liver and onions.

POTTS. That's him. I'm up doing all the Camden jukes. Three weeks
    running Luigi's light on his pennies. Every machine in Parkway is
    pulling in eight nine quid a week, Luigi's it's one bag, two, three
    quid if you're lucky. So I say stop having a chuckle, inky pinky
    blah blah blah you're gonna get a kidney punched out.

SWEETS. Only fucking language they speak.

POTTS. So he's gone, listen, he's gone 'No-one's playing the juke.'

SWEETS. Yeah right.

POTTS. He says. Nobody's playing it.

SWEETS. Like we're in Outer Russia.

POTTS. Like it's the *moon*. Outer Russia. Exactly. He says *they're doing it themself.* He says they've got a kid comes in here, gets up in the corner, does it himself. The fucking shake rattle roll himself. I mean. Camden kids?

SWEETS. Micks.

POTTS. Do me a favour.

SWEETS. Micks and Paddies.

POTTS. Do me a good clean turn.

SWEETS. Micks and Paddies and wops who fuck dogs.

POTTS. He says 'Come back tonight, you'll see.' So I come back tonight. And I take Ezra, Mickey we're gonna scalp him take the rig back he's told us a fib. (*Pause.*) Lo and behold.

SWEETS. No.

POTTS. In the corner, all the moves. Doing 'Sixty Minute Man'. Everyone watching. In the corner. A *child*. (*Pause.*) That's what happened. I'm not whining. I'm not bleating. You know, am I supposed to get back in the van start doing sums? 'I want xyz. Twenty, thirty, forty per cent.'

SWEETS. You're not some fuckin' vulture.

POTTS. I'm not some fucking *doorboy*. I want what's due. I want what's fucking mine. (*Beat.*)

   Enter BABY. *He stands there for a bit.*

BABY. Drinking wine spo-deeodee,
   Drinking Wine spo-deeodee,
   Drinking wine spo-deeodee,
   Dancing on a Saturday Night.

POTTS. Oh Watcha Baby . . .

SWEETS. Watcha Babes. How you getting on?

POTTS. How's it going down there? Anyone left?

BABY. Hello Sweets. What a night eh?

SWEETS. Yeah . . .

POTTS. How you feeling Babes?

BABY. Well Sid, actually I feel great.

POTTS. Yeah? You look awful.

SWEETS. Go and put your feet up. You look like a corpse.

BABY. Yeah. Well let's play then. Bring a crate up, relax, few disks
. . . Let's get it started.

POTTS. Yeah. Actually. We'll get it started later . . .

BABY. Oh. What's up?

POTTS. Nothing.

SWEETS. Nothing at all. No. (*Pause.*) It's just they're having a bit of
a meeting.

POTTS. No they're not.

SWEETS. Exactly.

BABY. What's going on then?

POTTS. Nothing. They're just relaxing.

BABY. What? In there?

POTTS. Something like that. It's nothing. Best keep the noise down.

BABY. Say no more Sidney. (*Laughs.*) Ssshhh!

SWEETS. Exactly. Sssh.

BABY. Look at that. We forgot the cake.

SWEETS. Yeah. That was my fault. I was supposed to take it down at
the last song, pass it around. Completely forgot.

BABY. Look at that cake. That is a brilliant cake. You better hide it
Sweets. Or you'll be in hot water.

SWEETS. Yeah I will. I'm gonna hide it.

BABY. Well. All right. I'm gonna go downstairs now.

POTTS. Brilliant.

BABY. Have a spruce up drink.

POTTS. Good idea.

BABY. Just to spruce me up a bit. You want to join me?

POTTS. Yeah. We'll be right down.

BABY. Sweets?

SWEETS. Yeah. I'm gonna be straight down.

BABY. All right. I'm going down now.

POTTS. Okay. See you in a bit mate. Play a game later.

BABY. Drinking wine spo-dee-o-dee. My piss is black.

SWEETS. It's the white ones. Don't eat no more of the white ones.

BABY. The white ones. (*Laughs.*) Spo-dee-o-dee. Sssshh!

Exit BABY.

SWEETS. Do you think he knows?

POTTS. What do you think?

SWEETS. Ezra wouldn't tell him.

POTTS. He couldn't find the gents in this place without asking.

SWEETS. Ezra wouldn't tell him. Ezra wouldn't trust him.

POTTS. Ezra wouldn't trust him to run a tub. He doesn't know.

SWEETS. If you don't know you don't know.

POTTS. Good. Good. The end. Sweets. I heard 'fifty-fifty'. (*Pause.*)

SWEETS. Okay. Say that again.

POTTS. I don't know.

SWEETS. Okay. Just that little last bit again.

POTTS. I don't know.

SWEETS. You heard fifty-fifty. You said you heard fifty-fifty.

POTTS. I don't know. Don't turn it into nothing. Don't knit a blanket out of it.

SWEETS. Okay. Stop. Sid. Think. Was it Sam? Did Sam say it?

POTTS. Tricky. With the smoke, I'm pouring tea bent double I heard those words. That word. 'Fifty.' Twice. Fifty. Fifty. Five-O. And the single word 'America'.

They look at each other.

SWEETS. Okay. Okay. Okay. All we know –

POTTS. All we know is 'Fish are jumping, and the cotton is high.'

SWEETS. Fish are jumping. Precisely.

POTTS. Good. The end. Talk about something else.

SWEETS. Exactly. Good. Great night.

POTTS. Great night. Exactly. We're fucking made.

SWEETS. My life makes sense.

POTTS. Go upstairs see if there's an angel pissing down the chimney.

SWEETS. My whole fucking life makes sense. (*Pause.*) Hold it. Hold it. We've not been told.

POTTS. Makes no difference.

SWEETS. Have you been told?

POTTS. Have you been told?

SWEETS. No.

POTTS. Makes no difference. Go to the museum.

SWEETS. Right. What?

POTTS. Go down take a look at any picture Napoleon. Go take a
butcher's at the Emperor Half the World. And you'll see it. You'll
see. They got a lot of blokes *standing around*. Doers. Finders.
Advisors. Acquaintances. Watchers. An *entourage*.

SWEETS. Big fuckers in fur boots. On the payroll.

POTTS. Napoleon's chums. And they're all there. Sticking around.
Having a natter. Cleaning rifles. Chatting to cherubs. Waiting.
Waiting for the deal to come off.

SWEETS. They weren't there they wouldn't have fuckin' painted
them.

POTTS. Just 'cos now he's got a big horse don't mean he don't need
chums. He's got big, they've put him on the big pony, his mates
go – 'Maybe Napoleon don't want us around no more. Cramping
him up. Holding him back.' 'Cos one thing Sweets. They've put
you in seal-skin boots told you you're Emperor, that's when you
need mates. 'Cos one day they're gonna lift you back out, stand
you in the snow watch your fucking toes drop off.

SWEETS. Listen. Okay. All we know –

POTTS. All we know is 'Fish are jumping, and the cotton is high'.

SWEETS. 'Fish are jumping.' Exactly.

POTTS. 'It's a Nice Day' and 'Oh look the Fish are jumping, and will
you look how high that cotton's got.' Good. Good. The end.
They're going back to his.

SWEETS. Tonight?

POTTS. Billiards.They're going to Sam's house for billiards.

SWEETS. Clover.

POTTS. Knee-deep. Thrashing around in it. God spoke to me last
night Sweets.

SWEETS. Doesn't surprise me an ounce.

POTTS. God, said to me, 'Do not be troubled Sidney for your ship is
coming in. Yours is the racey big cock-shaped one over there going
faster than the rest so just keep your mouth shut and wait.'

SWEETS. Doesn't surprise me an ounce.

POTTS. He's gone 'Keep your mouth shut, unless your nose is in the
trough, then open your mouth, and chew like fuck. That's all there
is chum.'

SWEETS. You know what God said to me last night? He goes, 'Sweets, There's no God, do what you will, good luck, end of message.'

POTTS. The way I see it it goes like this: Fuck God.

SWEETS. Precisely. Fuck him on a cloud.

POTTS. Fuck God if you know the king. Do you know what I mean? Fuck God if you only know someone knows someone knows the king. Because if you know someone knows someone knows the king, and you wait long enough sooner or later you're gonna get a sweet taste of the king's cock.

SWEETS. Good rule.

POTTS. Great rule.

SWEETS. There's got to be rules and that's a rule.

POTTS. He's got dyed hair.

SWEETS. Who?

POTTS. Sam Ross has got dyed hair.

SWEETS. You're kidding.

POTTS. He's took his hat off wham! Bright yellow dyed hair. Not blond or nothing. Yellow. Like a banana.

SWEETS. I never thought I'd know that. I never thought I'd know that detail.

POTTS. Sweets. Sweets. The shoes. The motherfucking *shoes* on the man.

SWEETS. Buckskin. Hand-stitched.

POTTS. Baby buckskin. Baby fucking hand-stitched buckskin.

SWEETS. Baby fuckin' buckskin handstitched by elves.

POTTS. Baby fucking buckskin.

SWEETS. Baby what? Who *knows*? (*Laughs.*) Eh? Who fucking *knows*?

POTTS. Something rare. Something rare and soft. Something young, can hardly walk, kill it, turn it inside out –

SWEETS. Unborn pony.

POTTS. That's the one. Still attached. Still in the –

SWEETS. Still in its mother's womb.

POTTS. Asleep in the fucking exactly. Wake it up, rip it out, lah-di-dah, pair of shoes. Bom. It's over. I'm going out.

SWEETS. You don't like it? Who cares? I'm fucking paying.

Feet on the steps.

POTTS. Don't say nothing. Fish are jumping.

SWEETS. The cotton is high.

Enter SKINNY *with a broom. He is seething, furious.*

SKINNY (*shouts*). You cheap fucking sweaty fucking . . . fucking . . . Jew . . . fucking . . . (*Pause.* SKINNY *lights a cigarette.*)

SWEETS. Alright Skinny? What's up?

SKINNY. Nothing. (*Pause.*) I'm leaving. I've had enough. I'm telling Ezra. I'm going to get a proper job. I'm going to work in a bank.

SWEETS. Oh yeah? Something gone wrong.

SKINNY. You know the one in the dress with the thing up the back? We're having a chat, she's up for it, and Baby swans up, stands in here, close, and he does the thing with the . . . Says the thing about bad breath. The thing about that I've got bad breath. About my breath being bad. I get fifteen minutes free time, yeah, enjoy the night before the coats start leaving and he gives it the breath. (*Pause.*)

I'm tickets at the door seven Saturdays in a row. Seven straight. 'Skinny, you're on the door.' 'Skinny you're on coats.' The juke's fucked, who finds a spanner greases up his new shirt? 'Skinny chum, mop this pile of sick up for two and six an hour.' Yeah? Meanwhile, right, what's he doing? What's he doing? Oh look, he's at the bar. Oh look, he's leaning on the fucking bar. Is that Alan Ladd? No. I don't think so.

POTTS. Come here. (*He does.*) Breathe. (*He does.*) Skinny, your breath smells beautiful.

SKINNY. Thank you.

POTTS. It smells like English roses.

SKINNY. What? Thank you. Thank you.

POTTS. It's a pleasure.

SKINNY. Start of the night about five people in here, he comes up behind me on the door squeezes my bollocks. Not playful. Really gripping. And you know when you're not crying but water comes to your eyes. (*Pause.*) Fucking night. What you doing up here?

POTTS. Nothing.

SKINNY. Fucking weekend. Where's Ezra?

SWEETS. He ain't here. He's gone home.

SKINNY. It's all right, you just sit up here have a natter.

SWEETS. They all cleared off?

SKINNY. That darkie's still down there dancing on his own.

POTTS. Chuck him out.

SKINNY. You playing a game later?

SWEETS. Dunno.

POTTS. We'll see.

SKINNY. Is Baby playing? Because I'm not playing if Baby's playing.

SWEETS. Skin. Pop up the Half-Wops, get us all a frothy coffee, come back, then we'll all play.

SKINNY. Okay. I'll go and get a coffee. I've had enough of all this. I'm going to get hurt. I might want to have children one day. (*Pause.*)

POTTS. Go up the Half-Wops, come back, we'll play.

SKINNY. Fucking weekend. My piss is black.

SWEETS. It's the white ones. Don't eat no more of the white ones.

Blackout. Drumming.

Act One, Scene Two

Upstairs at the Atlantic. SKINNY is tied with his hands around the back of a juke box, his pants round his ankles. BABY, naked from the waist up, wild, is wielding an old navy cutlass and screaming at SKINNY that he is going to die. The others are all appealing to BABY to stop, but BABY swings the cutlass around pointing it at each of them in turn. SWEETS gets up on the desk, still shouting as BABY pushes the point against SKINNY's cheek. Enter MICKEY.

SWEETS is the first to spot MICKEY in the doorway. He calls to BABY over and over, and after the music ends it is a full ten seconds before the din subsides and SWEETS is just calling 'Baby' over and over, his eyes shut. Having won BABY's attention, SWEETS indicates to the door.

BABY. Oh. Hi Mickey.

SKINNY. Mickey. Christ. Thank Christ.

BABY *puts the cutlass down.* MICKEY *walks to the blinds and opens them. Bright sunlight pours into the smoke-filled room.* MICKEY *opens the window. Sounds from the street.*

POTTS. Gonna be another corker Mickey. Look at all that sunshine.

SWEETS. Mickey mate. How hard is this eh? I try to tell him. I be like a dad.

MICKEY *just stands there.*

POTTS. How's your head cold Mickey?

SWEETS. Mickey, how's your head chum? You feeling better chum? Bit more like it eh?

MICKEY. Everybody having a good time?

POTTS. Looks bad doesn't it?

SWEETS. Looks dreadful. Tell me how bad it looks. Tell me.

POTTS. Last night Mickey! You should have *been* there.

SWEETS. You missed a *night*. Like everyone's birthday at once. Place looks like a palace.

POTTS. One word. Sequins.

SWEETS. I'm going to say one word now and it's just been said . . . The fucking Sequins.

POTTS. Sequin after sequin after sequin. Sequins on the walls. Sequins on the ceiling. Sequins round the bar.

SWEETS. Looks like Little Richard walked in and exploded.

POTTS. I was saying only just now, wasn't I Sweets. *Underwater* theme. 'Ezra's *Atlantic*'. See, we noticed. The whole joint sparkles like the Briny Deep. Like Neptune's cove.

SKINNY. Hold it. Hold It. I say 'Fuck the Decor'. I say back to the issue of Me Being Tortured.

SWEETS. Look, this sprung from, you know, from circumstances. Game of Cards. Few Drinks. Few laughs. Few pills.

POTTS. Great pills. Sweet's pills.

SWEETS. M'mum's pills. Slimming pills.

POTTS. You have to wolf hundreds but in the end . . .

SWEETS. So. Few drinks. Few laughs. Few pills . . .

POTTS. Then lots of pills.

SWEETS. Our big mistake.

POTTS. Giant Mistake. Turned sour see. Big up then a big dipper down. What's the word? Emotional.

SWEETS. Emotional. That's Mum. Thin as piss but so emotional.

POTTS. You're up then 'bing' – (what's the word?) 'Jivey'.

SWEETS. 'Antsy'. Antsy in the pantsy.

POTTS. Puts the big gorilla monkey on your back. So. Few pills. Pale Ale. Big hand, it's all tense, Skin here whips the King of Spades out his sock.

SWEETS. Clean out his loafer.

SKINNY. I swear. It fell on the floor.

POTTS. I miss it, Sweets missed it, Baby sees it, he's got Queens-over-eights. Nine fucking guineas lying panting on the table.

SWEETS. And the rest is history.

POTTS. Exactly.The rest mostly speaks for itself. So.

SWEETS. So. That's what happened. That's what happened up until now.

POTTS. Hold it. Hold it. (*Beat.*) My heart's stopped.

SWEETS. Breathe.

POTTS. I can't breathe. My heart's stopped.

SWEETS. Are you sweating?

POTTS. I got no pulse.

SWEETS. Take a white one.

POTTS. I already had a white one.

SWEETS. Have your feet gone dead?

POTTS. Check.

SWEETS. Prickly face?

POTTS. Check.

SWEETS. Pits pouring sweat?

POTTS. Check.

SWEETS. Take a white one.

POTTS. You said –

SWEETS. It's up to you. Take a white one or die.

POTTS. What about black piss?

SWEETS. You want to be dead or you want black piss? (POTTS *takes one.*) Put your arms above your head and pant like a dog. (POTTS *holds his arms above his head. He pants. Pause.*)

SKINNY. Mickey. What we were talking about in the van.

POTTS. Bingo. I'm back.

SWEETS. Welcome home. You should get a rush.

POTTS. I'm getting a rush.

SWEETS. Euphoria. Your body's glad it's not dead.

POTTS. She's going like a choo-choo . . .

SWEETS. You're glad to be alive.

POTTS. Great to be me. Great to be me. This is a fucking great time to be me. I'm all right.

SWEETS. Great night. Great night.

POTTS. I'm better than all right. I'm fantastic. Great night. Great night. Hey Mickey. Mickey. Guess what? I saw this bloke sick up in his bird's mouth.

SWEETS. I saw that.

SKINNY. Mickey. Enough. Remember what we spoke about in the van. And this isn't for me. It's for you. Fuck me. For you.

BABY. This is advice you're about to get Mickey.

SKINNY. Advice? Are you Italian now? No. You're not. You're a Jew. *Be* one.

BABY. He's pulling them out his shoes, I'll just lie down and take it eh?

SKINNY. It fell on the ground. It falls on the ground you pick it up.

POTTS. Baby. I think you have something to say to Mickey.

SWEETS. Yeah, c'm on Babes and we can all get on with our fuckin' lives. (*Pause.*)

BABY. Uh, Skinny. (*Laughs.*) What are you staring at?

POTTS. Charming. Charming. Baby –

SKINNY. Fuck off.

BABY. What, are you giving me the eye? Are you giving me the evil eye?

SKINNY. You nothing fucking piece of dog'splop.

SWEETS. Baby –

BABY. Because (excuse me Mickey). Because if you're giving me the evil eye you're doing it wrong.

SKINNY. I fuck your mother and she shouts your name.

BABY. Because you look like you love me. You look like you want to put your cock in my ear. Look away. Look away.

SKINNY. Fuck off. I'm not playing.

SWEETS. Drop it Baby. We're all a bit honky tonk.

BABY. Lookin' like you want to put your cock in my ear. Look away. Look at the floor.

SKINNY. Big man. Big man.

BABY. Look at the floor. Don't look at me. Look –

SKINNY. I'm going to get hurt here Mickey.

POTTS. Oh this is helping. This is fucking perfect for a tired man with head cold to come back to work to.

BABY. Sweets boy, put on something slow and evil. Mickey looks like he wants to dance.

SKINNY. This is it. Mickey. You see? It's *time* . . . (BABY *starts to leave*.) . . . Watch this. Watch this.

MICKEY. Baby . . . (BABY *stops*.) Where you going?

BABY. Well, Mickey, you know I thought I'd pop out and get a toffee apple. (*Pause*.)

SKINNY. A toffee apple . . . What does that mean? For me it means Mickey you take it up the bum with a toffee apple you let me walk out of here. I don't see how it could possibly refer to anything else. (*Pause*.)

MICKEY. Go out the front. Don't go out the back.

SKINNY. Brilliant.

MICKEY. Lock the door.

BABY. I don't have my key.

MICKEY. Where is your key?

BABY. I lost it. Dancing.

MICKEY. Don't go out the back.

BABY. How's your head cold Mickey? You feeling all right?

MICKEY. Did you hear me? Don't go out the back.

BABY. Oh. Mickey, I forgot to say. I love the sequins. They make the whole night sparkle.

Exit BABY. *They untie* SKINNY.

POTTS. Hard man act.

SWEETS. Nutter act.

POTTS. Complete fucking bollocks.

SWEETS. Giving it the stare. Complete fucking bollocks.

POTTS. You only do that when it's bullcrap.

SKINNY. Mickey, with the key bit. Did you hear? He lost it dancing
  ... Eh? And some people get trusted with keys some don't – You
  watch. Now we'll get the till nicked and we'll all stand around
  wondering how they got in. I get kicked in the shins, get my nuts
  squeezed. Now do something or don't do something but it's time
  to do something Mickey. It's time to do something.

MICKEY (*low*). Shut your fucking gob alright? Shut your fucking gob.

  MICKEY *snaps the blinds shut.*

SKINNY. I'm sorry? Are you talking to me?

MICKEY. What time did you leave?

POTTS. Whassup Mickey?

MICKEY. Shut up. What happened here last night?

SKINNY. That's fucking charming.

SWEETS. Relax Mickey. It all went like a clock.

POTTS. Look, Mickey you know what he's like, he's talks a lot. Chat.
  I'll make sure this don't happen again.

MICKEY. Fuck all this. You stupid cunt. We're finished.

SWEETS. It's not that bad. Take a minute to clear up.

POTTS. What's up Mickey.

MICKEY. What's up? What's up? Ezra's dead.

  Everything stops.

SWEETS. Something ... uh ... (*Pause.*) Something happen Mickey?

MICKEY. Yeah. Yes. Something happened. (*Pause.*)

POTTS. He's fucking *what*?

SWEETS. You said that Mickey. You said he's dead.

  Pause.

MICKEY (*trembling, quiet*). Jesus fucking Christ.

  Silence. Then, all at once.

OMNES. Oh Jesus. Jesus, Jesus fucking Christ.

Pause.

Jesus. Jesus Christ.

Pause.

SWEETS. What's happened Mickey?

MICKEY. I don't know.

Pause.

SWEETS. Okay. Can I ask you something? We're all going you know . . . going . . . bit honky tonk, and and and and and things are pretty going pretty fast here now to be honest and I feel you know I got my fucking heart flutters and everything –

SKINNY. Okay. Okay. Take it back. Take it back to before.

MICKEY. I got a call.

SKINNY. Are you sure?

MICKEY. I got . . . . of course I'm fucking sure.

SKINNY. Why didn't you fucking say?

MICKEY. It's . . . Why the fuck do you think? You're all sitting here going sixteen million –

POTTS. Mickey –

MICKEY. You're all . . . You fucking prick.

SKINNY. I'm sorry.

MICKEY. You're all doing six million miles an hour yap yap yap. You bunch of fucking children. Don't give me any mouth.

Silence.

SWEETS *puts his hands on his knees. He dry vomits.* POTTS *bends over and sticks his fingers down his throat.*

SWEETS. I got no sick.

POTTS. Put your . . . stick your fingers down your throat. Tickle that thing at the back.

SWEETS Got to . . . hang on.

POTTS. Tickle that bit that hangs down . . . the fuckin' . . .

SWEETS. I got no sick. I'll . . . just be a minute. Just get back on the flat.

SWEETS *and* POTTS *try to vomit. Nothing happens. Silence.*

SKINNY. What did they say Mickey? When they rung.

MICKEY (*pause*). They said 'You're finished.'

SKINNY. 'You're finished.'

MICKEY. They said 'You're finished' and 'Look in the bins'.

SKINNY. Okay. Okay. Okay. Okay. Okay. We're fucked.

Pause.

SWEETS. Jesus.

POTTS. Jesus Christ.

SWEETS. They say we're finished I believe them.

SKINNY. How do you know?

SWEETS. He got rung up this morning.

SKINNY. Yes. I know. Who by?

MICKEY. Alec Guinness. How the fuck should I know?

SKINNY. Mickey, who –

POTTS. How does he know? Eh? How does he know?

SKINNY. Mickey. Who off?

POTTS. People . . . fuck me gently . . . *People Ezra knows.*

SKINNY. Did they say who they was?

POTTS. No. No. Listen. (*Laughs.*) They don't tell you. They tell you it gives it away you catch them it makes it easy . . .

SKINNY. I'm not addressing you.

POTTS. Please. Please? Can I . . . Please . . . Someone he don't know isn't going to walk up do him for *fun*. He's not a fuckin' he's not some *slug*. He's not a fucking *spider* crawling across the floor.

SKINNY. Hey bullcrap, slow down. Open a window, take deep breaths. Relax, have a bubble bath. I'm talking to Mickey.

SWEETS. Warm milk. I need some warm milk.

Pause.

POTTS. All right. All right. All right. Stupid question Mickey . . . and Good. Let's ask questions. Stupid, brilliant, we don't know till it's asked. Exactly. Right. Good. *Are you sure?*

MICKEY. Am I sure what?

POTTS. I don't know. It's early. That he's dead. Good question. Eh? Mickey. Eh?

SWEETS. Good question.

POTTS. Eh? Eh? My question and it *is* a question is are you sure?

MICKEY. He's out there. (*Pause.*)

POTTS. Out where? Out the back?

SKINNY. Fucking hell. Now?

SWEETS. Fucking hell.

POTTS. It's a joke. It's Mickey's joke. It's Mickey's morning joke.

SWEETS. Out where?

SKINNY. Don't you listen? By the bins. That's what they said. 'You're finished' and 'Look by the bins'.

SWEETS. You said 'By the bins'. Mickey said 'In the bins'.

POTTS. By the bins in the bins. Is that the issue here? If it's 'by' are we safe? If it's 'by' is there a deal?

SKINNY. Mickey. Okay okay. Indulge me. Please. Are you sure? Are you ten times out of ten sure that he's passed away?

MICKEY. He's fucking cut in half. He's in two bins. (*Pause.*)

SKINNY. You hear that? Is it clear now? He is dead because they *fucking cut him in half.* So yes, he's fucking passed away. Allow Mickey to *know.* So. So. (*Pause.*) Sweet Fucking Hell Jesus and Mary.

POTTS. Fucking Nora. Fucking hell.

SWEETS. Suffering Jesus. They sawed him in half.

SKINNY. Poor fucking man.

SWEETS. You sweat your life away . . .

SKINNY. Poor fucking man.

SWEETS. Into a *bucket* . . .

SKINNY. Poor fucking man. Poor fucking man. (*Silence.*)

MICKEY. Fucking mess . . .

SKINNY. Poor fucking man.

SWEETS. Wake up have breakfast. They saw you in half.

MICKEY. Hideous fuckin' mess . . .

SKINNY. Poor fucking man. Poor fucking man. (*Silence.*)

POTTS. Sit down Mickey.

SWEETS. Sit down.

MICKEY. I'm all right. (*Silence.*)

SWEETS. Who's got a pill? Get a pill here for Mickey. Or a glass of warm milk.

POTTS. Mickey –

MICKEY. I don't want a pill.

SWEETS. We need a blanket. Shall I put some music on? Soft music?

POTTS. You fucking prick. Yeah, and we'll all have a slow dance till the coppers get here.

SWEETS. I don't know. I'm not someone's mum.

POTTS. Jeeesus.

SWEETS. Fuck off. I'm not someone's mother. I'm not Mickey's mum.

SKINNY. I said. I said. You make a stink you attract the big lights.

POTTS. It's done.

SKINNY. Make a stink you attract big lights. Make a stink you attract big lights. (*Pause.*)

POTTS. What the fuck does that mean?

SKINNY. You know . . . fuck off. You know what it means.

POTTS. Make a . . . What the fuck can that possibly mean?

SKINNY. Fuck off Sidney Potts.

SWEETS. Mickey. Mickey. Mickey. Let's talk . . . . Listen . . . Listen. Mickey. Listen to me now. Okay. Okay? Mickey. Charlie *Dodds*.

SKINNY. We'll . . . . Mickey –

SWEETS. Please. Please. Couple of pistols just to make me feel better. Please. Listen, please, as a precaut – Listen . . . Mickey . . . Mickey . . . Please. Just in case. In a drawer. Something. A safety net . . .

SKINNY. Mickey listen . . .

SWEETS. One or two. Just one or two pistols. You know? One or two in a drawer in a jacket. All we've got's an old cutlass. Let's at least try and make it fair sides.

SKINNY. We're gonna make this worse. We're gonna make this worse.

SWEETS (*overlapping*). Just *something* down here just so it ain't the fucking – just so it ain't the fucking Alamo.

SKINNY (*overlapping*). Sweets. Sweets. Sweets. Sweets. Sweets. Sweets. Sweets. Sweets. Sweets. Fuckin' *ease down* mate. Lie down. Lie down take deep breaths.

SWEETS. I'm fine.

SKINNY. Lie down.

SWEETS. I'm fine. I'm going to die.

MICKEY. Where's the kid?

POTTS. Sorry?

Pause.

SKINNY. Fuck the kid. This –

POTTS. Mickey –

SKINNY. Excuse me Mickey. But really. *Fuck* the kid.

MICKEY. Where is he? Where's the kid?

POTTS. Mickey –

SKINNY. This isn't about the kid. Mickey –

MICKEY. Is my question.

SKINNY. This isn't about Silver Johnny.

MICKEY. Am I Satan? Am I suddenly Satan? Am I Devil? Excuse me but I've been *robbed*. I've just had everything *taken away*. My fucking plans. My fucking everything. (*To* SKINNY.) Now I want some fucking answers. Now. Where is he Sidney?

POTTS. I don't know. Well I'm not in charge am I . . .

MICKEY. Did he leave?

POTTS. He'll be round his mum's. He'll be having a nap.

MICKEY. No-one saw him leave?

POTTS. Sorry. It's dark down there. Maybe you want the full story you should have been here. I don't know.

SKINNY. Hold it. Hold it. Mickey wasn't here. We were here. You were fucking here. You were here too so stop slinging shit.

MICKEY. Right. Right. All of you. Listen to me. Listen. What time did the kid come off?

SKINNY. Eleven. Sung Boogie Woogie Flu came off.

MICKEY. Eleven.

SWEETS. Just before. I didn't see.

MICKEY. And Ezra left?

POTTS. Yes.

MICKEY. Right. Right. Who with?

POTTS. No-one.

MICKEY. He left on his own?

POTTS. Entirely on his own.

MICKEY. Skinny, did you see him leave?

SKINNY. I was handing out the fucking coats for a change.

MICKEY. Right. Then you all came up here. It's. (*Pause.*) So I get called at eight say. That's five hours. And no-one heard nothing.

POTTS. What like.

MICKEY. What like? What like? Like someone sawing your boss in two outside the fucking window.

POTTS. We didn't hear nothing. We had the juke on.

SKINNY. You have to listen . . . Mickey, these are the people you got here. They fuckin' –

POTTS. I like the juke on.

SKINNY. They get it all day long they've got to listen to it all night.

POTTS. I like the juke on. You put on a quiet platter you don't expect to have to listen out for untold carnage in your fuckin' back alley.

SKINNY. You live in a dream world.

POTTS. So now I did it. I did it. It's all my fault Charlie Chan. You caught me straight off. I popped out to stretch my legs, bumped into Ezra, strolled around the back, and sawed him in two. Why don't we all kill each –

SKINNY. Listen you fuck –

POTTS. Yeah. Kill each other now make it fucking simple.

SKINNY. No-one stuck a fucking cutlass up your nose for breakfast did they? *You're* jumpy?

POTTS. Look at him getting on Mickey's side.

SKINNY. There are no sides. There's just our side and *them*.

POTTS. They just sawed one of us in two. I don't think I want to *be* on our side.

Pause.

SKINNY. Mickey, what do you think. Do you think we're finished?

Silence. MICKEY *takes his tie off and puts it on the desk.*

SWEETS. Mickey. There was something.

POTTS. Sweets –

SWEETS. He was talk – (*To* POTTS.) What?

POTTS. Can I speak to you? Please can I speak to you please. Aside for a tick. Please. Excuse me, Sweets Please.

SWEETS. What?

POTTS. Can I speak to you?

SWEETS. What?

POTTS (*quietly*). Do we know about this Sweets? I don't think we know about this.

SWEETS. They said. It's finished.

POTTS. Fish are jumping Sweets. Fish are still jumping.

SWEETS. It's *now*.

POTTS. We spoke about this. And it's not over. It's not over necessarily. You see?

SKINNY. Is this some game between you two?

POTTS. Sweets. My advice, please, and I've thought about this, is 'Shut the Fuck up'.

MICKEY. Tell me Sweets.

SWEETS. Um. (*Pause.*) I think maybe Mr. Ross was here. (*Pause.*)

MICKEY. Where?

SWEETS. Last night. We thought perhaps Mr. Ross was here last night.

MICKEY. Look at me. Look at me.

POTTS. Mickey –

MICKEY. Shut up. Shut your mouth.

SWEETS. We thought you'd been told.

MICKEY. Did you see him?

SWEETS. Well not exactly.

MICKEY. Hang on. What do you mean not exactly. What the fuck does that mean?

SWEETS. Sid did.

Everyone looks at POTTS.

POTTS. Okay. Okay. Okay. It's simple. Mickey. If you'll just give me thirty seconds and don't say anything because you don't want to get angry, I don't want to get angry, none of us does, we're all good ol' boys and all that so let's take it easy. Okay? Right. Now. It goes like this: What Sweets just said. It's a lie.

SWEETS. Sid.

SKINNY. What's going on?

POTTS. It's bollocks. It's not true.

SWEETS. Oh. Sid?

POTTS. That's – What? What?

SWEETS. It's just they said we're finished.

POTTS. (*Pause*) Shut up. *Mickey*. It's simple. What Sweets has said is not true. He *thinks* it's true but actually it's *not*. You see?

MICKEY. No Sidney. No I don't.

POTTS. Okay. Please. Please. Can I finish. Please? I know. I *know,* but. Hold on. Hold on. Exactly. Relax Mickey and I'll say.

SKINNY. I don't believe this.

POTTS. Hang on. Hang on. Mickey. Listen. This is my point. There was a chap here. But it weren't Mr. Ross.

SWEETS. Sam.

SKINNY. What?

SWEETS. That's his name. Sam Ross.

SKINNY. Oh for fuck's sake Sid.

POTTS. We don't know it was him. We – don't . . . excuse . . . Mickey. Some bloke called Sam. Could be Sam Spade. Sam Cooke. Sam Davis Junior.

Excuse me. Excuse me. I cannot put my hand on my heart and say yes I saw him. Because I've never clapped eyes on the man in my life, I'm working all night I'm full of pills, people coming and going. Faces. Saturday night. I'm like who's this, who's this, drink more, smoke more. Busy busy busy. Really can't say.

SKINNY. I don't fucking believe this.

MICKEY. What did he look like?

POTTS. Normal. Everyday.

MICKEY. Sweets, what did he look like?

SWEETS. I didn't see him.

MICKEY. What was he wearing?

POTTS. Usual. Trousers. Shirt. Jacket. Menswear.

SWEETS. And uh . . . Sid . . .

POTTS. What? What the fuck are you going to say now? What the fuck else might you possibly . . . hold on . . . Hold on. Shut up. What might you possibly wish to add?

SWEETS. Well . . . . About the fifty-fifty.

POTTS (*to* MICKEY). I don't know what he's talking about.

SWEETS. About them saying fifty-fifty.

POTTS. I didn't say that.

SWEETS. Oh. Right. I thought you did.

POTTS. That's not what I said. Mickey. I thought they *might* have. I thought they might have said fifty-fifty. I was excited. All right. I was excited and a bit honky tonk. It's not my business who comes here who doesn't. I take the tickets on the door and then I help clean up after. I drive –

SKINNY. Sid –

POTTS. I – Hang on. Hang on, because I . . . Some days I drive the van and I fix the machines. I don't front the place up. I hear a little rumour and I pass it on. That's me. I'm a cunt. Everyone knows it. So what? Doesn't make me Al Capone.

MICKEY. Sweets. Listen. Did he have yellow hair? (*Pause.*) I'm asking you. Did he have bright yellow hair?

Pause. MICKEY *walks up to* POTTS *and slaps his face.*

SWEETS. Oh fuck . . . Oh fucking Nora. We're dead.

SKINNY. What?

MICKEY. Is it locked downstairs?

SKINNY. Oh mothering Christ.

SWEETS. They're coming for us. Mr. Ross is coming for us.

MICKEY. What did I tell you? Look at me. What did I fucking tell you?

SWEETS. He had about three blokes with him earlier. They're all coming for us. Mickey. They had a meeting. They all came up here for a meeting.

MICKEY. Shut up. Now listen to me. Shut up.

SWEETS. They had a meeting. In there.

MICKEY. How many of them was there?

SWEETS. I don't know. He was with some others but they went home.

MICKEY. How many?

SWEETS. Three or four. Two with tattoos. One thinks he's all fashionable. Maybe a couple more. I couldn't tell.

MICKEY. Sidney, tell me what you saw.

POTTS. Fuck off.

SKINNY. Tell him Sidney. What happened.

POTTS. Fucking handing out the cuffs. Getting all cuffy when I'm over here trying my best. Fuck off.

SWEETS. Give over Sid, we're all bang in this now.

POTTS. Really helps that. I'm feeling really relaxed now.

SKINNY. We should have stuck to the jukeboxes. A good business. A safe business. A business you don't get sawn in half by Sam Ross.

SWEETS. Why don't you go and sing somewhere else?

SKINNY. When we were doing the jukes I can't recall any of us getting sawn in half. It's fucking when you when you include people. Look where it gets you. And I know you agree with me Mickey because I've heard you and Ezra in there.

MICKEY. Are you listening? Did they leave with Silver Johnny?

POTTS. Hold it. *Hold* it. It was fucking *busy*, we work here, it's the middle of the night it's packed and you're too ill to be here, I'm supposed to leave the party, leave the night in the middle of everything seek you out to report back some half piece of information ain't even our lookout. Sorry, I'm not doing my job, next time I'll know.Who made you Prime Minister anyway? I get my wage off Ezra and he's dead. I don't answer to you, and no-one else here does either. You have head cold. You weren't there so you don't know. You're walking in at the end.

Re-enter BABY.

BABY (*sings*). They call it a teenage crush,
    They can't believe it's real.
    They call it a teenage crush,
    They don't know how I feel. (*Pause.*)

SWEETS. Baby . . .

SKINNY. Mickey. Mickey . . . Mickey . . . Fuckin' hell. You know. Fucking hell.

MICKEY. Shut up.

SKINNY. You know? Fuckin' hell.

MICKEY. Shut up. All right? Shut up.

BABY *produces five toffee apples from behind his back.*

BABY (*sings*). They've forgotten when they were young.
    And the way they yearned to be free.
    All they say is the young generation
    Is not what they used to be.

He gives each person a toffee apple.

This is just for now. Tonight Skinny Luke I'm gonna buy you a drink apologise. I'm gonna buy Mickey a drink apologise. I'm gonna apologise to everyone.

SKINNY. Mickey . . . Baby . . .

MICKEY. It's all right. Baby, I call . . . . I got a call this morning. Somebody's murdered your dad.

> BABY *stands still. He puts his toffee apple down on* MICKEY*'s desk, walks around the desk and sits in the chair. They watch him.*

BABY. Guess what I just saw. (*Pause.*) Out there. Go on. Guess.

MICKEY. Baby –

BABY. Have a guess. Out there on Dean Street. Have a guess.

> *Silence.*

SWEETS (*quietly*). Some girl? (*Pause.*)

BABY. Wrong. Mickey?

MICKEY. I don't know.

BABY. Guess.

MICKEY. Baby –

BABY. Sidney? Have a guess.

POTTS. I don't know.

BABY. Have a guess. Have a guess.

POTTS. Tony Curtis. Give up.

BABY. Guess. No. Guess.

POTTS. Henry the Eighth?

> BABY *laughs at this. Pause.*

BABY. There's a *Buick* parked out there. A Buick in Dean Street. Right outside the Bath House. It's brilliant. (*Pause.*) Makes it look like Las Vegas (*With a soft G. Pause.*) Tonna kids hanging off it pretending they're . . . they're in a film. (*Pause.*) What's happening to this town? A Buick.

> *Silence.*

MICKEY (*to* SKINNY). Is it locked downstairs?

SKINNY. I'll check.

MICKEY. Go and check. Check the back and the front and check the windows. Check everything then come back up here.

SKINNY. I will. Mickey –

MICKEY. Check the windows check the doors. What?

Do that and come back up. Don't go outside.

SKINNY. Right. (*Pause.*) Baby, look, I'm sorry about before, I had the card in my sock. I'm sorry. I'm not . . . with the pills . . . (*Pause.*)

BABY (*to* SKINNY). Why didn't you say so earlier? I've just spent fivepence on presents.

SKINNY. What? Yes.

BABY. Toffee apples. Fivepence.

SKINNY. I know.

BABY. You cost me fivepence. Penny each. Five of us. Fivepence. You've just said sorry. You owe me fivepence for toffee apples.

MICKEY. Okay look –

BABY. It's your fault (hang on). It's your fault pay for the toffee apples.

SKINNY. I don't have it.

BABY. Borrow it off someone.

MICKEY. Baby don't mess around.

BABY. I think things should be fair round here now, or we'll all start wondering if we're getting done fairly. We don't want any hard feeling what with everything else do we. *Do* we?

MICKEY. No . . .

BABY (*to* SKINNY). Then pay me. Pay me. *Pay me*. (*Pause.*)

SKINNY. Mickey can I borrow fivepence?

MICKEY. Okay. Okay. Let's do this first. Because this is quite jolly. Are you having fun?

MICKEY *finds the money and makes to give it to* BABY.

BABY. Ah Ah. Not to me. To Luke.

MICKEY. Just take the money. Take the money.

Pause. He does, and puts it in his pocket.

BABY. I accept your apology Luke.

MICKEY. Check it's all locked up come back up.

SKINNY. I've got to talk to you Mickey.

MICKEY. Just do it. (*To* POTTS.) Bring the bins in.

SWEETS. Right. Mickey, I'm sorry. It's the pills. Warm milk we'll be fine.

MICKEY. Bring the bins up. Don't go out the front.

POTTS. Shall I help him?

MICKEY. Yeah. And give us a minute. Don't go out the front.

POTTS. Right. (*Pause.*) I'm sorry Baby. (*Pause.*)

BABY. Fucking night eh Sid?

POTTS. Yeah. Yeah. Fucking night.

> *Exit* SKINNY, SWEETS *and* POTTS. BABY *sits in Ezra's chair.* MICKEY *watches him. He picks up the cutlass and carries it into Ezra's back office. He re-emerges.*

BABY. You seen Luke's trousers?

MICKEY. What?

BABY. I go all the way to Monkeytown buy myself some stay-like-it twelve pleats. I walk around in them one week. Lo and behold Luke walks in here this morning it's like I'm looking in a mirror. And the red plims. Where's he got that idea from? Fucking twelve pleats and red plims.

MICKEY. Baby –

BABY. What? He copies my walk. I look over there, there's another me.

MICKEY. It's because he likes you.

BABY. It's because he likes me. Oh I know. He loves me. You know that smoke ring thing I used to do.

> *Pause.*

MICKEY. You need a sleep? (*Pause.*) When did you last sleep? Eh? (*Pause.*) Sid said someone was here last night.

BABY. Hold it. Hold it. If we're gonna talk business I don't feel right. If we're gonna uh . . . I'm not dressed right.

> BABY *takes* MICKEY's *tie, puts it on.*

MICKEY. Okay. We'll do . . . Fine. We'll do this later.

BABY. But it's working day. And I'm a working man.

MICKEY. Are you going to be *funny* about this?

BABY. I'm all ears.

MICKEY. You're all ears. You're all ears.

BABY. I'm all ears.

Pause.

MICKEY. Do you know who Sam Ross is?

BABY. Who?

MICKEY. Sam Ross. I know you know who he is.

BABY *sits there.* MICKEY *stands up.*

We'll do this later.

BABY (*overlapping*). Yes.

MICKEY *looks at* BABY. *He sits back down.*

MICKEY. Ross was here about the kid. He been after a part of the kid.

BABY. Oh yes? Which part?

MICKEY. He . . . Listen. Ross wanted to do a deal with your dad.

BABY. Over John?

MICKEY. Over . . . yes . . . Over Silver Johnny.

BABY. No-one told me.

MICKEY. I know you knew.

BABY. No-one told me.

MICKEY. I know you knew. Even Sweets knew.

BABY. No-one told me. This is fun. Two businessmen enjoying the morning.

Pause.

MICKEY. He was . . . Ross was saying he could get us into the halls, into the . . . into the cinemas. The money was going up. But . . .

BABY. But what?

MICKEY. Your dad weren't going to swap the kid for anything.

BABY. That's touching isn't it? (*Pause.*) We can do this later Mickey. If it's too upsetting.

MICKEY. Ross has got the kid. I don't know what the fuck has happened, I don't want any of this.

BABY. Mickey, I just drink the beer, have a laugh, kiss the girls and make them cry. Don't ask me.

MICKEY. They're going to come here . . .

BABY (*overlapping*). I wish I was more like *you* Mickey. I wish I was less like me, and more like you.

Pause.

MICKEY. *Listen to me.* They're going to come here.

BABY. They're going to come here.

MICKEY. Yes. I think they are.

BABY. Yes. I think they are.

MICKEY. If . . . listen.

BABY. If . . . Listen.

MICKEY. Baby –

BABY. Baby –

Pause.

MICKEY. You think you're in a book.

BABY. I am. I'm Spiderman.

Re-enter SWEETS *and* POTTS.

SWEETS. Mickey. I've just . . .

MICKEY. What?

SWEETS. Sorry. It's just I've just had a thought.

MICKEY. What?

SWEETS. Well it's just this. What about Ezra's Sunday Parlez-Vous?

MICKEY. What?

SWEETS. The Sunday . . . Ezra's Sunday Parlez-Vous. Everyone's gonna wonder why we're shut . . .

POTTS. What time is it?

SWEETS. Eleven. Says noon on the ticket.

POTTS. He's right.

SWEETS. There'll be a queue.

POTTS. I sold about a twenty tickets last night alone.

MICKEY. Listen.

POTTS. It's going to be very popular. We'll have a queue round the block in twenty minutes.

MICKEY. Listen. Listen. Fuck the Sunday Parlez Vous. I'll . . . *fuck* the Sunday Parlez Vous. I'll worry about that.

SWEETS. Yeah but Mickey, there's going to be a queue outside in ten minutes.

BABY. It's a problem Mickey. What are you going to do?

MICKEY. I worry about that. We'll put a sign on the door say we're decorating –

BABY. We just decorated . . .

MICKEY. I don't fucking care. We're doing it again.

Enter SKINNY.

SKINNY. It's all locked. There some kids hanging around out the front.

POTTS. It's the Par . . . . Mickey. What did I just say? Eh? It's the Parlez Vous.

SKINNY. What? Fuck.

POTTS. What did I just say?

SKINNY. Fuck. Is it Sunday?

POTTS. You watch. They'll flock.

SWEETS. Everyone was on about it last night.

POTTS. You watch.

SWEETS. That Sylvia, with all those mates. Knows those Mick builders.

POTTS. Who's suggestion was it? Eh? Turn Sunday, a dead day in the week, make it something. Who thought up the name. The continental feel. Who was it?

MICKEY. Sidney. Please.

POTTS. I'm just pointing it out.

MICKEY. I know. Just . . . Just keep the door locked they'll fuck off. Shut up. Just keep out of sight they'll all fuck off.

BABY. Skinny you look fantastic.

SKINNY. Sorry?

BABY. You look like a prince. Can I ask you a question? Where d'you get those trousers?

SKINNY. What? Oh . . .

MICKEY. Leave the trousers.

BABY. Aren't they lovely? With the pleats. Little turn-up. (*He looks down at his own and feigns shock.*) Well well. Small world.

SKINNY. Mickey –

BABY. Now I ask myself, where would you get a fashionable idea like that from?

SKINNY. Baby I never knew you had a pair. Mickey, I never knew he had a pair.

BABY. It's lucky that or people might think you were copying me. People might think you loved me or something.

SKINNY. I bought them over Monkeytown. I saved up.

BABY. You're a fucking liar Skinny Luke.

MICKEY. Baby go downstairs.

BABY. I'm gonna . . . excuse me Mickey . . . I'm gonna let you wear them so long as you kiss mine.

SKINNY. What?

BABY. I promise. I won't cause a fuss, if you just come over here and kiss my pegs.

SKINNY. Fuck off. Mickey –

BABY. Kiss my pegs.

POTTS. Here we go.

BABY. Kiss my pegs.

SKINNY. Fuck off.

BABY. I know why you say all those things about me. It's because you love me so much. Mickey says.

MICKEY. Baby, leave him alone.

BABY. It's because you're fighting with yourself. I know what I do to you Skinny Luke. Now show me. Kiss my pegs. Kiss them. (BABY *throws a chair at* SKINNY.) Look at the floor. Look at the floor.

SKINNY. Great fucking game. Great fucking game. Great fucking game.

BABY. Look at the . . . Look at the floor. I'll close your fuckin' eyes. Kiss my pegs.

SKINNY. Fuck off.

BABY. Kiss my pegs. Kiss my pegs.

SKINNY. Fuck off. Mickey –

BABY. Kiss my pegs. Kiss my pegs.

POTTS. Kiss his fucking pegs.

SKINNY. Throwing chairs Mickey. That's a new one. That's an escalation. What did I tell you about the pattern. Insults, spitting, squeezing, threatening. Throwing chairs. I'm going to end up dead Mickey. You watch.

MICKEY. All right. Calm it down.

SKINNY. I've had enough.

MICKEY. Skin listen. Go over Charlie Dodds.

SKINNY. I've had enough.

MICKEY. Shut up and listen. Go over Charlie Dodds.

SKINNY. Right.

MICKEY. Do you know where he is?

SKINNY. Who?

MICKEY. Charlie Dodds. Does the guns. Do you know –

SKINNY. Yeah. Yes. Old Compton up the top.

MICKEY. Get the best he's got. Go there come back. Don't talk to no-one. Don't get stopped.

SKINNY. Right.

MICKEY. Stuff it up your shirt down your trousers. Don't get fuckin' pinched.

SKINNY. What if I bump into someone?

MICKEY (*handing over money*). Act.

SKINNY. Right. And I'll get some sandwiches.

MICKEY. Listen. For fuck's sakes. Are you listening to me? Just go Charlie Dodd's come back here. Go now.

SKINNY. Right. I've got to talk to you Mickey.

MICKEY. Do it now then come back here.

SKINNY. Good. Good. I've . . . we'll talk Mickey. I might want to have children one day.

Exit SKINNY.

SWEETS. This is it. This is it. We're all going to die here.

MICKEY. We're not going to die. We're going to stay here, we'll be alright.

SWEETS. I'm scared Mickey.

MICKEY. It's alright. Go out the back get those old mattresses.

POTTS. Are we staying here?

MICKEY. Just get them.

SWEETS. Are you sure Mickey? That we're going to be alright?

MICKEY. Yes. I am. I'm sure it's all right. (BABY *gets up to leave.*) Where are you going? Baby.

BABY. I fancied a sandwich.

MICKEY. Stay here.

BABY. I'm hungry.

MICKEY. Stay here. Do you want to still be a part of this or not?

BABY. Do I want to be a part of this . . .? This is brilliant!

MICKEY. Because you are a part . . .

BABY. Is this an . . . an *invitation* . . .?

MICKEY. You're supposed to be a part . . .

BABY. Am I being asked? Am I being courted?

MICKEY. Look. I don't care what you do long-term, I don't mind. But for a couple days I need you here.

BABY. What for?

MICKEY. Because you're his son. It goes Ezra you me to the outside.

BABY. That's why I've been here? Decoration. Like the sequins.

MICKEY. They're going to come here. If not Ross, anyone wants this place. Now to the outside you're the son, so you're the man.

BABY. So why did they call you? (*Pause.*) Somebody decides to kill my daddy, do they call me tell me? No Mickey. They give you the call. (*Pause.*) You see what I mean Mickey? You got the call.

Re-enter SKINNY.

SKINNY. Mickey.

MICKEY. What the fuck is it? I sent you to do a job.

SKINNY. It's just I found this on the doorstep.

SKINNY *holds out a box, big enough to hold a football, gift-wrapped with a silver ribbon. He puts it on the floor in front of them all.*

POTTS. I know what that is. I know what that is.

SWEETS. What?

POTTS. I know what that is.

SWEETS. What is it?

SKINNY. Fucking hell.

POTTS. Oh no.

SKINNY. Fucking hell. Fucking hell.

POTTS. It's the kid. It's the fucking kid's head.

SKINNY. Oh Jesus.

POTTS. Look at it. What do you think it is. It's the kid's head isn't it?

SWEETS. Oh Jesus.

POTTS. It's the kid's head. It's the fucking kid's nut isn't it. Well isn't it?

MICKEY. Shut up.

POTTS. Look at it. Perfect size. It's his nut.

MICKEY. Shut up.

SWEETS. Look. It's his fucking head. It's his fucking head in a box.

POTTS. How heavy is it? Heavy. I bet it's about a couple of stone. If it's a couple of stone it's his nut. One two stone it's the nipper's nut without much doubt.

MICKEY. Shut up.

POTTS. Oh my Jesus. They cut his head off.

MICKEY. Calm down.

POTTS. They're going to kill us all.

SWEETS. My God.

POTTS. It's over.

MICKEY. Shut up. All of you. Shut up.

SKINNY. Just say if it is because I don't want to see. Just nod if it is.

POTTS. We're finished. We're finished.

BABY *goes to the box. He unties the ribbon and opens it. He stares into it, standing over it. He pulls out a silver jacket, folded up. He unfolds it and looks at it. He holds it up for the others to see. Puts it on.*

He goes to the jukebox, jingles his pockets, finds a penny, drops it in the slot, presses a number and a tune begins.

Rock 'n' Roll plays loud in the office. All eyes are on BABY. *He ties the silver ribbon round his head and begins to dance. He starts slowly, menacingly, quick steps, tight, arrogant. As the song builds he moves faster and faster until it has become a noise. The sound grows, the drums getting louder, the instruments in discord, the beat intensifies until it reaches fever pitch, a wall of sound. It grinds deafeningly as* BABY *gets closer and closer to* MICKEY *until he is right in his face. At its peak, everything stops except the drumming, with* BABY *frozen, staring into* MICKEY*'s eyes. They are staring at each other. The drumming halts. Tableau.*

Blackout. End of Act One.

Act Two, Scene One

Downstairs at the Atlantic. Sequins everywhere. A staircase up to the office at the back with a chain across 'Private'.

An enormous banner across the back reads 'Ezra's Atlantic Salutes Young People'.

BABY *is out cold at a table, wearing the silver jacket.*

MICKEY *talks on the telephone.*

MICKEY. I want Camberwell 7212. (*Pause.*) Hello? (*Pause.*) It's Mickey. I want to speak to Mr. Ross. To Sam Ross. Yes. Yes I'll wait.

Enter SWEETS. MICKEY *puts the phone down.* SWEETS *walks back out and re-enters dragging a dustbin, followed by* POTTS, *also dragging a dustbin.*

MICKEY. Is the back locked?

POTTS. I've put the bolt on.

MICKEY. That bolt's too weak. A kid could break it in. Where's Skinny?

SWEETS. He's not back.

POTTS. Look. It's gone six.

SWEETS. Count on it Mickey. He's fucked it up.

POTTS. You sent the wrong bloke. Probably had his collar felt five pistols down his pants.

SWEETS. Who you calling Mickey?

MICKEY. A band for next week. Tell me when he wakes up. (*Heads towards office.*)

SWEETS. Mickey. Can I have a quick word?

MICKEY. What?

SWEETS. Had a little idea.

MICKEY. What is it Sweets?

SWEETS. Quick little tetty over here . . . (MICKEY *waits.*) Can I? Good. Lovely. (*Pause.*) You know that business earlier with Sid. I know he's sorry. It was the pills.

MICKEY. Forget it. None of us is ourself.

SWEETS. Couple of days we'll all be us again, go for a drink crack jokes about it, eh?

MICKEY. What was your idea?

SWEETS. What?

MICKEY. You said you had an idea.

SWEETS. Good. I've come up with a plan and it makes sense to me in my head, but before you answer, mull it over for half a minute, live with it a tick then see if I'm wrong. Okay? So: (*Pause.*) I say we all do a runner. (*Pause.*)

MICKEY. Sweets –

SWEETS. Mull it over Mickey.

MICKEY. Is that it?

SWEETS. Sounds obvious but the best ones always do. We've had a shock lah-di-dah who says we all of us put it behind us jump on a train. All of us, as a team, train down Margate splash in the sea. (*Pause.*)

MICKEY. Baby wakes up let me know.

SWEETS. Give it half a minute watch it grow on you. The cool sea breeze. Cure-all. Works wonders for head cold. What?

MICKEY. We've got no lease on this place. We've got no deed.

SWEETS. Right . . . .

MICKEY. It gets out about Ezra anyone who wants this place can walk in make themselves at home.

SWEETS. Uh-huh.

MICKEY. So we go down Margate, lark around, come back find it's gone. Then we've lost it all.

SWEETS. Absolutely.

MICKEY. So we're gonna stay here sweat out the weekend. See what happens, hopefully Monday it's still ours. After that, I don't know.

SWEETS. Horse sense. Twenty-four carat.

MICKEY. You see?

SWEETS. Mickey, go in there, close the door, lie down, let the dirt drop out your fingernails. Any news we'll give you the holler.

POTTS. There's a hole in your plan Mickey.

MICKEY. Oh yeah Sidney. Tell me.

POTTS. This. What if Mr. Ross comes back? (*Pause.*) Eh? Sam Ross gets his strength back comes here finds we hung around. What next?

MICKEY. Then I don't know. (*Pause.*)

SWEETS. You don't know?

MICKEY. No.

SWEETS. Think about my plan Mickey. It's got something. Sun. Donkeys. Kiss Me Quick . . .

MICKEY. Nothing's keeping you here Sweets. You want a piece of what's left, okay; you want to go out in the sun get an ice-cream, go to Margate you're welcome. Train goes from Victoria. (*Pause.*)

SWEETS. Mickey come over here and piss all down my leg. How far do we go back? Don't . . . How far do we go back?

MICKEY. I know.

SWEETS. I walked in the old warehouse can I have a job I'll work for fuck all. Come over here and piss all down my leg.

MICKEY. I'm proud of you Sweets.

POTTS. Mickey. Do you think he's going to come for us?

MICKEY. You've met him Sidney. You tell me.

MICKEY *goes up the staircase.*

POTTS. What?

SWEETS. What? Nothing.

POTTS. I thought you said something.

SWEETS. No. Me? No.

POTTS. Handing out the cuffs. Fucking getting cuffy. I didn't start all this.

SWEETS. He's as shook up as any.

POTTS. My ears still ringing.

SWEETS. I know. Wake up tomorrow you'll be right as rain.

POTTS. We're not waking up tomorrow. You heard what he said. He hasn't got a plan. What if I cuffed him. That'd be it wouldn't it? But no. I'll just stand there line up let you all have a swing. (*Pause.*) He tries it again I'm gonna start thumping back. And hard as I can.

SWEETS. Relax Sid. Have some cake.

POTTS. Who fucking discovered the kid?

SWEETS. Right.

POTTS. Fact. One solid gold forgotten fact.

Pause. BABY *stirs in his sleep.*

SWEETS. Poor bastard.

POTTS. I shouldn't worry about him too long Sweets.

SWEETS. Don't you feel a pang for him?

POTTS. I've got my own plate of shit to eat today thank you. I don't even know this hurts him.

SWEETS. Big heart Sid. 'Course it hurts him.

POTTS. Mickey first says it to him, Sorry Baby but your dad's been done. What does he do? He gives it the Buick. Some sketch about a car in the street. (What he's already told you and me the day before, the same fucking words.) Now chop my old man up see if I stand around swapping car models.

SWEETS. Yeah but there's dads and dads. You're thinking of a *dad*. Like in a book. Fucking figure of something.

POTTS. Yes but –

SWEETS. Not some bloke waits for you come home home from school stuffs his hands down your pants. Not one has you biting the sheets and then don't tell your mum.

POTTS. Don't get me wrong. I like him. I'm not saying I'd run back in and save him the building catches fire but he's a mate. He's one of my best mates isn't he? But he's a cunt. Oh. He's had it tough. Oh. His dad did the funny on him. Well that's all the past isn't it. Fucker's dead. He ought to draw a line now. Start afresh. But he won't. I know he won't. The trouble with his type is they think the world owes them a big kiss and a trip down the zoo. (*Pause.*) Have you got any pills?

SWEETS. I've run out.

POTTS. Thank Christ for that.

Enter SKINNY.

SKINNY. Relax. Panic over. You sweat for nothing and suddenly it's okay. Sweets you are a genius. This is your town. (*He removes a Derringer purse-pistol.*) Can you see that? Can you just *make that out*?

SWEETS. Christ.

SKINNY. A Derringer.

POTTS. Marvellous . . .

SKINNY. An antique . . .

POTTS. Sweets . . .

SKINNY. A collector's item. A curiosity.

SWEETS. Where d'you get that?

SKINNY. They crash in here it turns sour I'll gun them all down.

POTTS. Brilliant.

SKINNY. Mow 'em all down go up the Nellie Dean.

POTTS. Marvellous.

SKINNY. Five quid for the week off Charlie Dodd. Our private angel over Old Compton Street.

POTTS. Fuck. It's a sign.

SKINNY. It is. It's a sign. It says 'We are the men with the small gun'.

SWEETS. Did you say you was with me?

SKINNY. Yeah. Yeah. Yes. Yeah. 'Sweets Who?' (*Beat.*)

SWEETS. Cunt.

POTTS. That's a big hole in the plan then.

SWEETS. My brother had two Webley's off him last March.

SKINNY. Bow and arrow we've got the set.

SWEETS. Colin did. Pair a Webleys.

SKINNY. Have you bolted the back?

POTTS. What's the point? A kid could break in. Hang on. How did you get in?

SKINNY. Mickey gave me the key.

POTTS. When?

SKINNY. Last night. When he said I was in charge. I'm going to go and check the back. Come back find you all dead.

Exit SKINNY. *Pause.*

POTTS. Did you know that?

SWEETS. I had no idea. (*Pause.*)

POTTS. Do you believe him?

SWEETS. He's got the key. (*Pause.*)

POTTS. This, Sweets, is very bad for us.

SWEETS. What the fuck is going on?

POTTS. He's got the . . . Mickey gave him the key.

SWEETS. Big mistake. Mickey's made a big mistake there.

POTTS. I'm disappointed. I'm disappointed in Mickey.

SWEETS. It explains a lot. The whole . . . the –

POTTS. Minute we turn our backs – 'Mickey can I help you with this.' Mickey let me shake the *drips* off. Before, right, before it's this is wrong with the club, that's wrong with the club, and and and as soon as soon as there's aggro he runs under the fucking shawl.

SWEETS. Don't waste any time do you Missy . . .

POTTS. You watch, they'll share a fucking mattress tonight. And with the . . . with the Charlie Dodds. Who suggested that eh? Who suggested it?

SWEETS. Me.

POTTS (*beat*). Exactly. And who gets packed off. Who gets trusted? You and me? Now . . . Now he'll walk in here and he'll want us all to kneel down kiss his crack.

SWEETS. With all the ordering us about with the mattresses. Like it's a scout camp . . .

POTTS. Getting into it. This isn't a fuckin' fresh air fortnight. This is real.

SWEETS. Thinking he's in the trenches –

POTTS. Giving it the Uncle Tommy –

SWEETS. The fucking Uncle Tommy –

POTTS. We're gonna get the Uncle Tommy. We're gonna get the Uncle Tommy. (*Pause.*) Fucking mess we're in.

Re-enter SKINNY.

SKINNY. Where's Mickey?

POTTS. See?

SKINNY. Where is he. (What?)

POTTS. Never you mind love.

SKINNY. What?

SWEETS. He's upstairs.

POTTS. He's got his head cold.

SWEETS. He's got his head cold doesn't want bothering. What's it like out there?

SKINNY. Beautiful. Sunny. There's a few kids out there. Stupid bastards are queueing up.

SWEETS. Yeah. tell 'em the shows round Mr. Ross's tonight.

SKINNY (*i.e. the bins*). This him then?

POTTS. Yeah.Yeah that's him.

SKINNY. Fucking hell. (*Pause.*) You had a look?

POTTS. You haven't got the stomach.

SKINNY. A quid.

POTTS. Done.

SKINNY. Here. Half a crown and a Bazooka Joe.

POTTS. Done. (*They shake.* SKINNY *readies himself. He can't do it.*) Shitter.

SKINNY. It's harder than you think. (*He gives* POTTS *half a crown and the Bazooka Joe.*) I don't fucking like this.

POTTS. Don't you feel bad about it? What with it all happening on your first night in charge. Not a pretty start, is it?

SKINNY. Fuck off.

POTTS. Saps your confidence though I bet. As a leader.

SKINNY. I'm not listening to you. (*Pause.*)

SWEETS. Poor man. One minute he's up on the stage. Introducing. Doing all the introducing. In his blue suit. His best blue suit. His little joke at the start. (*Pause.*)

SKINNY. We should have stuck to the machines.

POTTS. Here we go. What was that Skipper?

SKINNY. What? Ezra never saw straight again the day the kid walked in here. Buying him silver suits. Wearing tight trousers himself. I mean an old man wearing tight trousers. It's asking for trouble.

SWEETS. That's true.

SKINNY. Eh? Thinking I am in love all's well in the world. Thinks if he combs his hair puts on tight trousers it's All Hail the Prince of Clothes.

POTTS. You're all heart Skin.

SKINNY. Just because some old man wants to fuck children for a hobby don't mean we all have to die in his good name.

SWEETS. He was always level to us weren't he Sid.

POTTS. Treated me fair. Played the gent.

SWEETS. Poor man. I'll miss him. (*Pause.*) All right. Here's a good bet. Which half's his legs and which half's his head?

POTTS. Ten bob says left one's his head.

SWEETS. I reckon left.

SKINNY. Yeah you've picked 'em up.

POTTS. Yeah but we haven't looked.

SKINNY. Null bet. Null bet.

POTTS. Jeeez. Nice to be trusted.

SWEETS. You should be a bit more trusting.

SKINNY. I watch my back all right.

SWEETS. You should be a bit more trusting my son.

SKINNY. I watch my back all right. (*Pause.*)

POTTS. You get any sandwiches?

SKINNY. Mickey gave me a fiver. I spent it on a small gun.

SWEETS. Eat the cake.

POTTS. I've eaten the cake.

SWEETS. Eat the cake. It's got . . . It's the same as bread.

POTTS. I eat any more of the cake I'm going to die. I'm going to turn blue die of cake poisoning.

SWEETS. It's the same as bread.

POTTS. The cherries. They're wax. They taste like wax.

SKINNY. Chuck a bit over then. (Blue icing . . .)

POTTS (*to* SWEETS). Look at this . . .

SKINNY. What.

POTTS. Am I the cake fetcher?

SKINNY. I'm asking you – Just gimme a piece.

POTTS. Am I your cake fetcher?

SKINNY. No. No. You're not. Absolutely. You jumpy cunt. I thought we were mates.

POTTS. Would you get *me* a piece of cake?

SKINNY. Mates. Friendship. You know?

POTTS. Would you fetch me cake?

SKINNY. I thought we were mates.

POTTS. We're business friends.

SWEETS. I'll get you some. You want some of the cake?

SKINNY. Grow up.

SWEETS. I'm sorry?

SKINNY. No.

SWEETS. What did you say?

POTTS. He said 'Grow up'.

SKINNY. I don't want to play.

POTTS. He said 'Grow up'.

SKINNY. I don't want to play that's all.

POTTS (*to* SWEETS). You see?

SKINNY. What?

SWEETS. Fucking Victor Mature.

POTTS. Fucking coming-of-age party.

SKINNY. You two live in a dreamworld.

POTTS. Whereas you have a long flowing beard.

SKINNY. A world of your own.

POTTS. You have the long whiskers of wisdom.

SKINNY. You know nothing about the real world. My Uncle Tommy was in the R.A.F, yeah, and when they were pinned down, and some, say someone said, here Tom, Tommy, fetch me a bit of cake or a cuppa tea you did it because of team spirit.

POTTS (*to* SWEETS). With the Uncle Tommy . . .

SWEETS (*to* POTTS). Do you hear that?

POTTS (*to* SWEETS). What did I say . . .?

SKINNY. What?

POTTS (*to* SWEETS). Fuckin' Uncle Tommy who won the war on his own.

SKINNY. It's true . . . they helped each other out. Someone says can I have a cup of tea –

POTTS. Uncle Tommy and his Halifax bomber. Uncle Tommy who shot down Hitler. Uncle Tommy who pinned down the bosch single-handed at the Somme.

SKINNY. He fought in both World Wars.

POTTS. Here we go. And they're off.

SKINNY. What? Fuck off. He fought in both World Wars. He said he was older than he was in the First and younger than he was in the Second.

SWEETS. And he had four brothers and they all died in action at the Somme.

POTTS. Shame.

SWEETS. Four older brothers mind.

POTTS. I bet they did it on purpose. I bet they did it on purpose to get away from Uncle Tommy.

SWEETS. Fucking . . . Skin, give Uncle Tommy a call get him round here and when Sam Ross gets here he can kill him for us.

SKINNY. I'm not listening to you. I asked you for a piece of cake. You just have no understanding of history. Those people died for you.

POTTS. Are you still here Sunshine. Why don't you fuck off and join up.

SWEETS. Join up fight the jippos. Take your little gun. See if they'll have you.

SKINNY. You have no understanding of history. (*Pause.*)

SWEETS. There's toffee apples.

POTTS. I know there's toffee apples. Stop fucking toffee appling me.

SWEETS. They're good.

POTTS. Fucking mess we're in. (*Pause.*)

SWEETS. Anyway, why's he called your Uncle Tommy when he's shacked up with your mum?

SKINNY. Fuck off. I'm not listening.

SWEETS. Eh? Sid. *Uncle.*

POTTS. Fucking friendly uncle.

SKINNY. I'm not listening. (*Pause.*)

POTTS. Fucking mess we're in.

Enter MICKEY *from the upstairs.*

MICKEY. What did Charlie say?

SKINNY. Mickey. I'm sorry. He only had this.

POTTS. Might as well give Sam Ross a Chinese burn as pop him with that. Waste of Sam's time.

SWEETS. He's got more. I know he's got more.

POTTS. Mickey, sorry but you sent the wrong bloke.

SKINNY. He doesn't even know you.

POTTS. That's nice Skin. Mickey gives you a job, you walk around in the sunshine, fuck it up, come back point the stinky finger at Sweets.

SWEETS. It's got a lovely bone handle.

MICKEY. Give it here. (MICKEY *takes the gun.*) All right. Don't worry. We've still got the cutlass.

SWEETS. Where is it?

MICKEY. It's up there.

SWEETS. Shouldn't we have it out here? Handy.

MICKEY. Leave it. Have you eaten?

POTTS. Mickey, it's about the cake. I can't actually eat any more or I'm going to sick up.

SWEETS. It's the same as bread.

POTTS. We need some supplies. You're in charge. What next?

SKINNY. Mickey, can I have a word?

MICKEY. What about? (Eat the cake).

POTTS. Sorry. It makes me gag.

SWEETS. There's toffee apples.

SKINNY. Mickey –

POTTS. Fucking leave it with the toffee apples.

MICKEY. For tonight it's the cake. We'll get something else in the morning.

SWEETS. Mickey, what do you suppose he's doing right now?

MICKEY. Who?

SWEETS. Silver Johnny.

MICKEY. I don't know. He's with Sam Ross.

POTTS. He's on a plane to Acapulco with Sam Ross. He's sitting in a bubble bath. I know he is. Right now up to his scrawny neck. Eating a goose off a floating platter.

MICKEY. He's got a big fat smile across his face I can tell you that much.

SWEETS. Do you know what I think? I think he's had all his teeth covered in silver, and he's got silver plated hair and nails, silver feet and silver pubes and he's singing at the Washington Bowl with loads of famous people watching. (*Pause.*)

SKINNY. Mickey?

MICKEY. What?

SKINNY. Can I have a quick word? It's private.

MICKEY. What is?

SKINNY. The quick word. Can we go up there?

MICKEY. Okay. Go up. (SKINNY *goes up the stairs.*) Tell me when he wakes up.

Exit MICKEY *up the stairs.*

POTTS. Stick a pin in me.

SWEETS. If I hadn't seen it . . . .

POTTS. Did I fall asleep miss the wedding?

SWEETS. Bad for morale that. Very bad.

POTTS. You know he can stand in the corner down here clicking his fingers being big with the twelve-year-olds waving like he don't drive the van. He drives the van and I say he should drive the van.

SWEETS. Standing at the bar like he don't drive the van.

POTTS. In the corner with the twelve-year-olds . . .

SWEETS. And . . . and . . . and . . . With the fuckin' –

POTTS. The fucking American.

SWEETS. With the American accent.

POTTS. Honestly. It's sad.

SWEETS. To girls. In this stupid American accent.

POTTS. He sounds Welsh.

SWEETS. Getting snug.

POTTS. Cuddling up to Mickey . . . this is wrong that's wrong. With his fucking bunch of keys.

SWEETS. . . . . Fucking bad breath –

POTTS. Fucking bad breath van boy. Fucking bad breath van boy with chat.

BABY *suddenly sits up. He sits there, not moving.*

POTTS. Here we go.

SWEETS. Hello Colonel. How's that?

POTTS. Bit more like it eh?

SWEETS. Now that feels a lot better don't it.

POTTS. Sweets, get Baby a glass of water.

SWEETS. How you feeling Baby-o. Ready for the party?

Pause. BABY *sits there.*

BABY. What time is it?

POTTS. What? It's the evening.

SWEETS. July. Lovely long evening.

POTTS. Still hot. Long shadows down Dean Street I bet.

SWEETS. Lovely out. Must be.

POTTS. Boiling hot. Skin said.

BABY. Yeah? (*Pause.*) I miss anything?

POTTS. Yeah. There was a wedding.

SWEETS. Yeah. Mickey and Skinny got hitched.

POTTS. Whirlwind romance. Very touching.

SWEETS. That's the cake over there. Potts was best man and I sung the carol.

BABY. Where's is he?

SWEETS. Mickey? He's up there mate.

POTTS. Up there with the lucky lady.

SWEETS. He's up there bumming him off right now.

POTTS. Yeah. He's bumming off his bad breath van boy bride. So. Mickey don't love us any more. That's what's happened. That's all you missed. (*Pause.*)

BABY. You know it *is* a hot evening. I can smell it on the breeze.

POTTS. Yeah.

BABY. Yes. I can smell it. Like when you're a kid and you wake up and it's summer.

SWEETS. Typical eh? Rains all July, then the day they chop your boss up you go into hiding, wouldn't you know, a scorcher.

POTTS. Shut it Sweets.

SWEETS. Absolutely. Sorry Babes.

POTTS. It's the cake. He's eaten nothing but cake for ten hours.

SWEETS. It's the blue icing.

POTTS. Relax. (*Pause.*)

BABY. So who wants to go up the pictures?

POTTS. That'd be the one wouldn't it. Normal Sunday have a cold lemon go up the Curzon.

SWEETS. Fuck about after up St. James.

POTTS. Maybe head down Monkeytown. Hang out.

SWEETS. Town's your oyster.

BABY. What about it? Quick flick. Eh? Quick Bob Mitchum.

POTTS. Yeah. Sorry Babes. Can't.

SWEETS. Love to Babes. Not allowed.

BABY. Come on. Who wants to go and see a Wild West?

POTTS. I personally would love to. But Mickey's decided it. We're all stopped here.

BABY. Who says?

POTTS. Mickey says.

BABY. Mickey says.

Pause.

There's probably kids outside.

SWEETS. Skin said there's a few.

BABY. Shall we get them in. Open the bar?

SWEETS. We can't mate. Love to. Can't.

BABY. Oh. (*Pause.*) Sidney, quick film?

POTTS. All right Baby. Stop pulling my cock.

BABY. What?

POTTS. You know we ain't going out, having a party, doing a conga, nothing. We're staying here. Why? Because of what's in those bins. Blunt as it is, I've had nothing but sorrow and birthday cake since sun-up, so stop the Music Hall. All right love?

SWEETS. Relax Sid.

POTTS. I'm relaxed. I'm talking.

BABY. This him?

He lifts the lid off one. He looks. He puts it down. He lifts the lid off the other. He looks, then puts it down.

Sweets?

SWEETS. Yes Babes?

BABY. I think I'll have that glass of water now please.

SWEETS. I'll just get you one.

Exit SWEETS.

POTTS. Fucking weekend. You feeling all right?

BABY. Tell the truth I'm a bit tired.

POTTS. Yeah?

BABY. Yeah. Feel . . . . tired like when you see old people and they look tired. You know what I mean?

POTTS. You'll pick up. It's the shock. (*Pause.*) You shouldn't have done that.

BABY. What?

POTTS. Had a look. You'll only have a bad dream now. I remember when I was four I saw this dog get ripped up by these pykies. They had it tied up on a swing and they had these pinking shears and a rake. (*Pause.*) Carried that little doggy round in my head for weeks.

BABY. Yeah. Maybe I'll have a bad dream or something. (*Pause.*)

POTTS. You should hear what Skinny was saying about you Babes. (*Pause.*)

BABY. About me?

POTTS. What?

BABY. You just said.

POTTS. Yeah. He was saying stuff to Mickey. About you.

BABY. What about me?

POTTS. How now's the time to brush you off.

BABY. Did he say that?

POTTS. Fucking bad breath . . . He opens his mouth something uncouth plops out.

BABY. What did he say then?

POTTS. He saying to Mickey he reckons we should brush you off. That blah blah pissing on we don't need the Jew no more.

BABY. Ah . . . He doesn't mean that.

POTTS. He said it. Something like it . . .

BABY. He doesn't mean that. He only says that because he loves me.

POTTS. Yeah? They're up there right now. Luke and Mickey. He's fucking got his feet nicely under the table.

BABY. I take no notice. I know it's just because he wants to walk like me. You all right Sid?

POTTS. Me? Tops.

BABY. You look white.

POTTS. It's the pills. I'm crampy. My stomach's all shrunk.

BABY. Your tummy? Does it hurt?

POTTS. It's like a lump of stone.

BABY. You had a sleep?

POTTS. What? No. I can't.

BABY. You should have a sleep Sid. I'll keep watch.

POTTS. Go downstairs stick your head under the tap. Clear your thoughts. (*Pause.*) I'm fucking shitting myself Baby.

BABY. Ah I shouldn't worry. Mickey's got it all under control.

POTTS. He ain't even got a plan. Besides, they made him God I missed it. Fucking getting cuffy with me.

BABY. He hit you?

POTTS. Right on my eardrum. It's ringing.

BABY. Mickey hit you? Did he hurt you?

POTTS. What? Not bad. But it knocks you back you get a cuff.

BABY. I'll say. That's not like him.

   Re-enter SWEETS.

SWEETS. Here you go. Nice chilly drink.

POTTS. You run it for a bit? The nippers climb up there slash in the tank. Always run it count to six.

BABY. Thank you Sweets.

   BABY *drinks the water.*

SWEETS. You ever seen him before?

BABY. Who?

SWEETS. Mr. Ross.

POTTS. Fucker's a legend South of the River.

SWEETS. Last year. Last year, when the Billy thing. Billy the . . .

POTTS. The Billy thing.

SWEETS. The fuckin' Billy thing. The fucking Billy the Bass.

POTTS. The double bass –

SWEETS. The double Billy thing. The stand-up bass player. Getting his own –

POTTS. Says he wants –

SWEETS. About his own manager. Shows up one night he's got his own manager along. He's the *bass player*. What happens? Eh? I'll tell you what happens.

POTTS. To the manager. This is the Hyde Park –

SWEETS. They find him lying in Hyde Park. I'll tell you what happens. They find him lying in Hyde Park.

POTTS. (. . . fuckin' . . .)

SWEETS. They find him *twitching* in the Park.

POTTS. (. . . fuckin' . . .)

SWEETS. They've woken him up driven up the Hyde, staked the fucker out and and and and and –

POTTS. The lawn –

SWEETS. . . . and drove a lawnmower over him. Over his face. Drove a lawnmower over his face.

POTTS. Fuckin' hell.

SWEETS. Over his face.

POTTS. Fuckin' hell.

SWEETS. Lawnmower. Over his face.

POTTS. Fuckin' hell.

SWEETS. The bloke's a vegetable.

POTTS. He's chopped liver.

SWEETS. His face is chopped liver.

POTTS. (. . . a pool of its former glory . . .)

SWEETS. A mockery of its former self. Then they've had breakfast, gone round the bass player's and they've cut his thumb off.

POTTS (*simultaneous with 'cut'*). Cut his fucking thumb off.

SWEETS. Lah-di-dah – they've cut his fucking thumb off. Round his mum's. In front of his mum. Him in his Jimmy jams.

POTTS. (Pyjamas.) Thereby depriving him of his livelihood.

SWEETS. Thereby depriving him of his *thumb*. The livelihood speaks for itself.

POTTS. You do that and it can speak for itself.

SWEETS. Then exactly.

POTTS. Good.

BABY. I don't know him no. But I'd like to meet him.

POTTS. Yeah? Well it looks like you're going to get the chance my son.

SWEETS. I know one thing. He comes back here I'm over the roofs and in Stepney before he's had time to get his saw out again.

Re-enter SKINNY *and* MICKEY.

POTTS. So what's he like?

SKINNY. What?

POTTS. You ought to brush your teeth more.

SKINNY. What?

POTTS. Me? Nothing. What's that smell?

SKINNY. What are you talking about?

POTTS. Mickey, can I say something. As it's all up in the air, I'm a bit jumpy, Sweets is a bit jumpy, can we have the little councils down here in the open. Not up there with the cutlass. I mean I love you both but I'm a bit scatty with the pills and I might get the hump kill you both in your sleep. I'm not saying you're planning nothing but my mind might be damaged. You never know. (*Pause.*)

MICKEY. You all right Baby?

BABY. I'm fine thank you Michael.

MICKEY. You feel better?

BABY. Sweets here got me a nice drink of water.

SWEETS. He's looking the part now.

BABY. Mickey, can I have a word with you?

MICKEY. What?

BABY. In private.

MICKEY. What do you want to say?

BABY. It's not for everyone to hear. It's like . . . (*Laughs.*) It's private.

MICKEY. Baby –

BABY. Seriously, I want a word.

MICKEY. Anything you want to say, say it to us all.

POTTS. Hang on. Hang on. Do I have to point out the fucking obvious here?

SKINNY. What?

POTTS. Giving me the what? Mickey. *Come on.*

MICKEY. What's your problem Sidney?

POTTS. Why don't I tell you. I get a thump in the head Skinny gets a massage upstairs.

SWEETS. Let's all take a step back.

POTTS. You should hear the stuff he says when you're not here.

SKINNY. I do not.

POTTS. Mickey should have done this . . . Mickey fucked this up, Mickey knew all about the deal did nothing.

SKINNY. Mickey I did not.

POTTS. He did. He said you knew all about Sam wanting the kid and you done nothing.

SKINNY. He's lying Mickey.

MICKEY. Sid, relax.

POTTS. I'm not happy Mickey. My ear's still ringing.

MICKEY. I'm . . . listen. Relax. I'm sorry I hit you.

POTTS. I've got some things I could say. I've got some ideas.

MICKEY. I know.

POTTS. I'm not happy Mickey.

MICKEY. Just relax Sidney. Everyone knows you're here.

BABY. Mickey, I want to say sorry. (*Pause.*) Uhhh. (*Pause.*) All right. I think . . . . Well. (*Laughs.*) I know I don't do much to run things, in the past. And I haven't like . . . . Well, I've decided to buck myself up. Make improvements. Because I want to stay round here, and I think if we're going to uhh . . . . Well, that's it.

MICKEY. It's still too early for –

BABY. No. I'm serious. I've thought about it.

MICKEY. I'm pleased.

BABY. I know what you must think. But you know, there's nothing like someone cutting your dad in two for clearing the mind. (*Pause.*) I do think that, what with my making improvements, I should be allowed to be more of a help to you Mickey. As if we were going to run things together. I mean, obviously you're in charge, but we could like run the club together. Like I could tell people that we run it together. Do you know what I mean?

MICKEY. I'm glad you've thought about it. We need you here, like I said.

BABY. I know. And I know why and I understand. I'm happy with that. I mean, where else would I go eh? Where else would I have this much fun?

MICKEY. Baby, I'm going to make you a deal. You don't dance me around, you leave Skinny Luke alone, then you help out a bit more then in a week we'll talk. That's all I'm gonna say.

BABY. I want to try.

MICKEY. You do that, you leave Skinny to get on with it, we're in business. Yes?

BABY. Okay.

MICKEY. You start squeezing his nuts I've got a problem. Because he's a good little worker, and he's telling me now he's walking out of here you give him any more niggle.

BABY. You said that.

SKINNY. I've just had enough Baby. I want us to get along.

BABY. Skinny, I'm sorry. I'm not going to squeeze your nuts any more.

SKINNY. It's just it really hurts. I might want kids one day.

BABY. I'm sorry.

MICKEY. Right. What time is it?

POTTS. It's sunset. Getting cooler.

MICKEY. All right listen. Skinny, bring up the other mattresses. Bring up some of the painting covers and stuff, make some blankets and things.

SKINNY. Right.

MICKEY. You two, take some full beer-barrels from in there, push them up against the back door.

SWEETS. Right.

MICKEY. Baby, give them a hand.

BABY. Okay. Uh. Mickey.

MICKEY. What?

BABY. What are you going to do?

MICKEY. I'm making a call.

BABY. Right. I've had an idea.

MICKEY. What's the problem?

BABY. I think maybe you should give them a hand.

MICKEY. Sorry.

BABY. I think you should. With the barrels.

MICKEY. That didn't last long then did it?

BABY. No. No. Hang on. It's just . . . What are you going to do?

MICKEY. I told you.

BABY. What was it again?

MICKEY. I'm going to make a fucking telephone call.

BABY. Who to?

MICKEY. What do you mean who to?

BABY. Just who might you have to call?

MICKEY. I've got to call a band.

BABY. Which band?

MICKEY. What do you mean what . . . . a band that was gonna play here Tuesday lunchtime.

BABY. Right.

MICKEY. An oldies' band.

BABY. I'll tell you what Mickey. You help them. I'll make the call.

MICKEY. I'm sorry?

SKINNY. Mickey –

MICKEY. It's all right. What do you want to prove Baby?

BABY. Nothing. I just think you should carry the barrels. Pushing them up against the door. It's a good idea.

MICKEY. You want to make a big deal out of the first fucking thing we do?

BABY. No. No. I just think we should start like it's all fair, and you should help with the barrels.

MICKEY. I've asked you to.

BABY. And I've asked you to.

MICKEY. Have you finished being hilarious? Because if you have I've got a phone call to make.

BABY. What's the number?

MICKEY. Fuck off.

BABY. Tell me. Tell me the number. What's the big deal? It's only a phone call. Don't you trust me to make a phone call?

SWEETS. Baby –

BABY. What? Mickey, listen, if Ezra asked you to carry the barrels, what would you do?

SWEETS. Me and Sid can manage the barrels. You put your feet up.

BABY. Mickey. You know? If Ezra asked you what would you do? Because the other day Ezra asked you to stick five thousand sequins all over here and you crawled round on your hands and knees all day. You did. I saw you.

POTTS. Babes that ain't going to help.

BABY. What? I don't see the problem.

MICKEY. It's all right Sid.

BABY. What's the difference now? Just imagine I'm Ezra. (*Pause.*)

MICKEY. All right Baby. You're the boss. Tell me what you want me to do. Why don't you tell us all what we're going to do? (*Pause.*)

BABY. Are you serious?

MICKEY. I'm waiting. Tell us all your plan.

BABY (*laughs*). All right. Who wants to go and find the blowjob?

POTTS. Don't fuck around Baby.

BABY. I'm serious. Why don't we all chip up Sam Ross's let him know how we feel. Let him know we're not happy and all. I reckon we ought put up a bit of a struggle. What do you reckon Sweets? All chip up at Sam Ross's door ask for him back. (*Pause.*) Skinny. Fancy it? That's not very Dunkirk of you. I bet your Uncle Tommy would be game.

SKINNY. Baby, just do this and it will make Mickey happy.

BABY. What?

SKINNY. What?

MICKEY. Go upstairs Skin.

SKINNY. What did I say?

MICKEY. Just go upstairs.

SKINNY. What did I say? What . . . Mickey? What did I say?

   Pause.

BABY (*quietly*). Kiss my pegs.

SKINNY. Fuck off.

BABY. Kiss my pegs.

SKINNY. Fuck off. Mickey –

BABY. Do it. Kiss my pegs.

SKINNY. Two minutes. Two minutes and we're off again.

BABY. Kiss my pegs. Kiss my pegs.

POTTS. Baby.

BABY. Kiss my pegs.

   Skinny. What did I say?

POTTS. Kiss his pegs.

SWEETS. Kiss his fucking pegs . . .

BABY. Do it. Do it. Do it.

MICKEY. Baby, why do you do this. Go upstairs cool off.

BABY (*to* SKINNY). Fucking get rid of me you cunt . . .

MICKEY. Go upstairs.

   BABY *stops. He goes upstairs.*

SKINNY. That's it. I'm off.

MICKEY. Skinny –

SKINNY. I've had it Mickey. I'm going to get hurt I stay here.

SWEETS. Just wait down here. He's in shock.

SKINNY. Fuck shock. He's a nutter.

POTTS. It's an act. He's a bullcrap. Go up there, punch him in the face, he'll turn into Little Bo Peep.

MICKEY. Skinny. Stay down here.

   But BABY *is coming back down out with the cutlass.*

POTTS. Here we go.

SWEETS. Oh for fuck's sake Baby. Who do you think you are?

SKINNY. Now I'm going to get hurt. Now he's going to kill me.

POTTS. He's not going to kill no-one. It's bullcrap.

SWEETS. Don't shame yourself up Baby. Put the sword down. Look. Just stand there. Million pounds says he doesn't.

SKINNY. Sorry but that's not enough.

POTTS. We can do this again or we shift the barrels. That bolt won't hold.

BABY. Kiss my pegs.

SKINNY. All right. I'll do it.

POTTS. No you won't.

BABY. Do it.

POTTS. Tell him to fuck off.

SKINNY. Fuck off. I'll do it.

MICKEY. Baby. Get out.

BABY. I'm sorry? (*Pause.*)

MICKEY. I'm sorry for you, but I don't want you around here any more.

Pause. BABY *is taken aback. He laughs.*

BABY. That's not very nice.

MICKEY. Just go.

BABY. I see.

MICKEY. I hope you do. I hope you do. I'm sorry, but I want you to leave. (*Pause.*)

BABY. Now?

MICKEY. Yes. Now.

BABY. Right now. This second.

MICKEY. Yes. (*Pause.*)

BABY. Uh, Mickey.

MICKEY. I'm not listening to you Baby. You've fucked around here for too long. I'm sorry.

BABY. I've always liked you Mickey . . .

MICKEY. Leave. (*Pause.*)

BABY. Oh. Mickey. You've . . . you're so . . . you're a very decisive person aren't you. I mean, you've always been a bit of a dark one, a bit of a Mrs. Mopp for my dad and now . . . Well, you're showing qualities aren't you. You surprise me.

MICKEY. I'm sorry. I'm not going to ask you again.

BABY (*pause*). Mickey. (*Pause.*) Watch what you say to me.

MICKEY. I don't think I have to. I don't think any of us do.

BABY. This is my dad's place. And there's . . . I'm his son. There must be deeds, and it passes on to me.

MICKEY. There's no deeds. You'd ever opened a drawer here you might know that.

BABY (*quietly*). Well. (*Pause.*)

Be-bop a lula she's my baby, be-bop-a-lula I don't mean maybe . . .

Pause.

Be-bop-a-lula, she-hee-hee's my Babuh, mah babuh. Mah Babah.

Very long pause. On and on. BABY *stands around. He lifts the cutlass and holds it over* MICKEY.

MICKEY. I don't believe you Baby.

BABY *stands there. In the end he lowers the cutlass.*

Now fuck off. And don't come back.

BABY *stands there. He leaves. Pause.*

SWEETS. Jesus.

POTTS. Mickey –

MICKEY. Put the barrels against the back door.

SWEETS. What? Right. Come on Sid.

Exit SWEETS *and* POTTS.

SKINNY. Mickey –

MICKEY. Skin, get the sheets.

SKINNY. Right. Thank you Mickey.

MICKEY. Get the sheets.

SKINNY. It's really got to me. I've been sleeping bad.

MICKEY. Use all the ones don't have paint on them. You can tear them up into . . . well, you know.

SKINNY. Leave it to me Mickey.

MICKEY. And check all the doors and windows. You finish that, help the others.

SKINNY. Right. Mickey. Where are we sleeping tonight?

MICKEY. You can sleep down here.

SKINNY. Good. Good. I just thought we could sleep up there with . . . altogether. I just thought it would be better if we were altogether.

MICKEY. Okay. Take the mattress up.

SKINNY. Is that alright?

MICKEY. Take them upstairs. Yes.

SKINNY. Thank you Mickey. I'll sleep better.

MICKEY. I've got to make a call.

SKINNY. Okay. Thank you Mickey.

MICKEY. Do the sheets.

Exit SKINNY. MICKEY *is alone. Enter* POTTS, *holding a large bowl with a cloth over it.*

POTTS. Mickey old son? I made you this.

MICKEY. What is it?

POTTS. For your head cold.

Beat.

MICKEY. Right.

POTTS. It's hot from the steamer. Strictly you need friar's balsam but I've bunged in a couple gills of crème de menthe. It's all spearmint or something. All does the trick on your pipes.

He sets it down.

MICKEY. I'm fine. Do the barrels.

POTTS. It doesn't hurt or nothing. You stick your head over, breathe it all in, fixes you up in minutes. Come here.

MICKEY. I'm all right.

POTTS. Nonsense Mickey, come here.

MICKEY *goes to the table and sits down.*

MICKEY. What do I do?

POTTS. You just breathe. You just put your head over it and breathe. Short while you'll feel like a baby. You'll be clear as rain.

MICKEY *puts the cloth over his head and breathes.*

I'm going to do the barrels now. You just stay there Mickey. All right? (*Pause.*) Just breathe Mickey.

Exit POTTS, *leaving* MICKEY *alone, breathing in the steam.*

Blackout.

Act Two, Scene Two

Downstairs at the Atlantic. Hanging upside-down in the middle of the room, gagged, is a young man, wearing silver trousers and a pink shirt. This is SILVER JOHNNY.

Perched on a bar stool opposite is BABY, *wearing the Silver Jacket and drinking beer. There are empty beer cans on the bar. The shotgun is across his knees.*

BABY. . . . I was about nine, bit younger, and my dad tells me we're driving to the country for the day.

He's got this half-share in this caff at the time, and it was doing really badly, so he was always really busy working day and night, so like, this was totally out of the blue.

So I got in his van with him, and we drive off and I notice that in the front of the cab there's this bag of sharp knives. And like, a saw and a big meat cleaver.

And I thought 'This is it. He's going to kill me. He's going to take me off and kill me once and for all.' And I sat there in silence all the way to Wales and I knew that day I was about to die.

So we drive till it goes dark, and Dad pulls the van into this field. And he switches off the lights. And we sit there in silence. And there's all these cows in the field, watching us. And suddenly Dad slams his foot down and we ram this fucking great cow clean over the top of the van. And it tears off the bonnet and makes a great dent in the top, but it was dead all right. See we'd gone all the way to Wales to rustle us a cow. For the caff.

Now a dead cow weighs half a ton. So you've got to cut it up there and then. And I was so relieved I had tears in my eyes. And we hacked that cow to pieces, sawing, chopping, ripping, with all the other cows standing around in the dark, watching.

Then when we'd finished, we got back in the cab and drove back to town. Covered in blood.

Pause.

Do you know why I'm called Baby?

Pause.

Take out the papers and the trash,
Or you don't get no spending cash;
If you don't la la la la la,
You ain't gonna rock 'n' roll no more
Yackety yack, don't talk back.

(*Pause. He drinks. Pause. He laughs.*) Yackety yack don't talk back. (*He laughs, he gets up and walks around.*) Yackety yack don't talk back. (BABY *laughs. He moves the chair to right in front of* SILVER JOHNNY *and sits down.*)

So, like . . . (*Pause.*) So like when you met Little Richard, what were you gonna say? (*Pause.*) 'Evening Richard . . . I . . . '
(*Pause.*) 'Evening Little. Can I call you Little?' 'Sure, if I can call you Silver.' (*Pause.*) Seriously, you must have had some pretty nifty plans. What did you have planned? Were you going to go to Niagara Falls. Just you, Sam and the majestic spray.

Pause. BABY *clicks his fingers along to a tune in his head. He stops. He drinks. Pause.*

Do you think I'm good-looking? Seriously . . . No come on, I mean . . . Do you think I'm quite good-looking? (SILVER JOHNNY *nods helpfully.*) Seriously. Am I, like . . . am I would you say rugged or striking? (*Pause.*) Hold on. Am I rugged? (SILVER JOHNNY *shakes his head.*) I'm not. Am I striking? (SILVER JOHNNY *nods.*) I am . . . You think so.

BABY *finishes his drink, crumples up the can and puts it in the pocket of the Silver Jacket. He searches through the other pockets of the jacket. He finds a guitar pick.*

What this? Is it a . . . . guitar pick? Plectrum. Is it a plectrum? (SILVER JOHNNY *nods.*) Do you play the guitar? I didn't know you could play guitar. Can you play it? Seriously? (SILVER JOHNNY *shakes his head.*) Then what have you got this for? (SILVER JOHNNY *doesn't respond.*) What am going to do with you blowjob? Eh? What am I gonna do with you? (*Pause.*) What am I going to do with you?

Enter SWEETS *with the Derringer.*

SWEETS. Who is it? Who's there?

BABY. Who's that?

SWEETS. I've got a gun. Don't move.

BABY (*quietly*). Sweets. My man. You should be asleep.

SWEETS *is half way down the stairs. It is dark and he can't see* SILVER JOHNNY.

SWEETS. Oh. Watcha Baby. We thought you'd gone.

BABY. Ah . . . you know . . . I thought I'd drop by.

SWEETS. Right. How are you?

BABY. I thought I'd pop back in. (Fine, yeah).

SWEETS. What time is it?

BABY. No idea. Must be . . . . You been asleep?

SWEETS. Yeah . . . we're all . . .

BABY. Must be nearly morning. It was getting light out.

SWEETS. Yeah?

BABY. Gonna be another beautiful day. What you doing up so bright and early?

SWEETS. Oh. I'm supposed to be on watch.

BABY. What for. Baddies?

SWEETS. Yeah. Something like that.

BABY (*pointing to Derringer*). The fuck is that?

SWEETS. This? It's a . . . you know Charlie Dodd?

BABY. Yeah . . .

SWEETS. It's off him.

BABY. Give it here.

SWEETS. It's shit.

BABY. Give it here.

SWEETS. Wouldn't scare a kid.

BABY. It looks like a Turkish Delight.

SWEETS. Yeah. (*Pause.*) Baby, can I ask you a question?

BABY (*points it at* SWEETS). Fire away.

SWEETS. Right. Um . . . How did you get in here?

BABY (*stops*). I came down the chimney. Like Father Christmas.

SWEETS. Right. Right. We never thought of that.

BABY. No. No. You know my key. The one I lost dancing.

SWEETS. Yeah.

BABY. Yeah? Well, I never lost it dancing. It was in my shirt pocket
all that time.

SWEETS. Right. Right.

BABY. I found it. I had it all the time. In here. (*Beat.*)

SWEETS. Yeah actually, because I've been writing you a letter.

BABY. *You* have?

SWEETS. Yeah. Sounds a bit daft saying it like that.

BABY. What does it say?

SWEETS. Well, I've only just started it. It's just you know all that stuff
Mickey said. Well I, for one and I think certainly Sid, right . . .
Anyway. Just to say I don't really agree with Mickey on that one.
I think he's wrong.

BABY. Thank you.

SWEETS. Because we've always been mates.

BABY. We have. Yeah.

SWEETS. And, you know Mickey's like chucked you out. Yeah.
Well, as far as I'm concerned we should still go for drinks and
stuff. I mean, who knows what's round the corner? And I bet
Mickey changes his mind. Between you me and the lamp post.

BABY. Yeah?

SWEETS. What? Yeah. Yeah. Who knows? Who knows eh? What the fuck . . .

BABY. Yeah . . . Thing is Sweets, that's really nice and all, but the thing is I've always thought you were a bit of a tosser. (*Pause.*)

SWEETS. What? Oh.

BABY. Yeah. I've always had you down as a right nasty little cunt underneath. Like, all sweetness and light to your face, and then as nasty as can be in the real world. Also, you're not very bright, and I think you only hang around Sid all the time because you want his cock up your arse. (*Pause.*) You know? To be frank.

SWEETS. Right. Well. What the fuck eh? (*Pause.*) I don't you know . . .

BABY. Don't what?

SWEETS. He's just a mate. (*Pause. The penny drops.*) You rotten bastard.

BABY. Aaaaahhhh!

SWEETS. You dirty shit.

BABY. I got you sunshine.

SWEETS. You dirty bastard. You had me there.

BABY. Your face.

SWEETS. I was thinking, What? What's he on about.

BABY. You should have seen your face.

SWEETS. You dirty bastard. I twigged though.

BABY. You went grey in the face.

SWEETS. I knew pretty soon.

BABY. You need a drink after that don't you.

SWEETS. Telling me. You rotten git.

BABY. Drink?

SWEETS. Fuck it. Why not. Mickey comes down I'll just tell him you forgot something.

BABY. Is it a problem?

SWEETS. What? No. I'll just give him a spiel. Lovely.

BABY. Ice?

SWEETS. There's no ice.

BABY. What? There's always ice.

SWEETS. Not today.

BABY. No pills. No ice. Place is falling apart.

SWEETS. Yeah . . .

BABY. I turn my back for half an hour, place falls down round our heads. Let's have a look . . .

SWEETS. Ezra's in there actually.

BABY. What? In here.

SWEETS. Actually. Yes.

BABY. In with the ice?

SWEETS. Yeah. It was my idea. Just until further notice.

BABY. Both halves?

SWEETS. Yes. No. The legs are in the Frigidaire.

BABY. In the Frigidaire up there?

SWEETS. Pretty much.

BABY. Well, best leave him. Cheers.

SWEETS. Lovely, (Cheers).

BABY. To Ezra.

SWEETS *has seen what is hanging in the middle of the room.*

BABY. Top up?

SWEETS. What? No. No. Cheers.

BABY. You sure?

SWEETS. Uhhhh . . . (SWEETS *takes in the scene. He looks at* BABY, *at* SILVER JOHNNY, *everything is very quiet in the glow for ages. Then he bellows.*) Mickey!! Mickey!! Mickey!! Mickey!! Mickey!!

BABY. Ssssh. Quiet. Keep it down. You want to wake up all Soho.

SWEETS. Where'd that come from?

BABY. Keep it down. What?

SWEETS. Where d'you get that?

BABY. Oh, you know.

SWEETS. We thought –

BABY. Say hello to Sweets, John. You remember Sweets. The Sweets Man. Does the pills.

SWEETS. What's going on? I'm lost.

Enter POTTS *from down the stairs.*

POTTS. Sweets? You all right?

SWEETS. It's . . . look.

POTTS. The fuck is all the clatter?

BABY. Sidney Potts coming down the stairs there. Bet you never thought you'd see his ugly mush again.

POTTS. Baby. We thought you'd gone.

SWEETS. He still had his keys Sid.

BABY. Sidney. We've got four of us . . . we can have a little party.

POTTS *has seen* SILVER JOHNNY.

POTTS. Suffering Shit.

SWEETS. Precisely.

POTTS. Sweet Georgia Brown.

BABY. Do you like it?

POTTS. Where the fuck did you dig him up from?

BABY. What do you think?

POTTS. That is him isn't it. (POTTS *looks through his legs upside down.*) Baby, you fucking champion.

SWEETS. We thought he was in America.

POTTS. Will you look at this. Will you look what is hanging up there.

SWEETS. I don't understand.

POTTS. The one and only Johnny Shiny.

SWEETS. I'm lost.

POTTS. Okay. Okay. Baby. I'm catching up. I don't get it but so far I like it very very much.

BABY. You want a drink Sid?

POTTS. Yes. Yes. I do want a drink. I want a big drink. And I think we should talk because this makes a different story.

SWEETS. Get Sid a drink.

POTTS. My fucking . . . . right. Right. Back to plan one. Fish are jumping. Fish are jumping again. (*To* SILVER JOHNNY.) First things first. You little upside down queer bastard. The shit you're in. Had us sitting around filling our pants. You little wanker, Sweets here shat his pants because of you.

SWEETS. I didn't. It was the pills.

POTTS. Right. Good. I'm waking up. I'm awake.

BABY. Do you like it?

POTTS. Yes. I like it. I like it very very much. But. But. One thing. What the fuck is going on?

BABY. He was on the telly. I went round the back, opened it, and got him out.

POTTS. Baby. Okay. Listen. This changes a couple of things. First of all, you're my hero.

Enter MICKEY *and* SKINNY. MICKEY *remains on the stairs, overlooking the scene.*

SKINNY. Fuckin' hell.

POTTS. Eh? Feast your eyes Skinny Luke. Feast your eyes.

SKINNY. Where d'you find him?

POTTS (*to* SILVER JOHNNY). You fucking little bastard, not so fucking croony now are you? You better get used to that chain because it ain't coming off chum. I'm keeping you on that from now on.

MICKEY. What the fuck have you done?

BABY. Hello Mickey. You asleep?

MICKEY. What have you done Baby?

SKINNY. I don't understand.

POTTS. Mickey. Hello. Welcome. I think you've got a couple of things to say to our friend here.

SKINNY. . . . Fuckin' 'ell . . .

POTTS. I thought . . . Oy . . . Go upstairs . . . Crawl back under Mickey's blanket, do something else, I'm talking to Baby.

SKINNY. Fuckin' hell. It's him. Mickey, it's him.

POTTS. Makes you think doesn't it. We're all in here crouched down Baby goes out and does a day's work. Does what he can for us. And Skinny, it's not sweeping up and it's not fixing jukeboxes. It's saving our fucking everything. A real day's work.

MICKEY. Baby, where did you find him?

BABY. Sorry, Mickey?

MICKEY. You heard me.

BABY. Ah, he was round Sam Ross's. (*Pause.*)

'If your man ain't treatin' you right,
Come up and see you Dan,
I rock 'em roll 'em all night long
I'm a sixty-minute man.'

SKINNY. What's going on Mickey? Baby, what have you done?

BABY. Well, I left here and I walked around for a bit and then I sort of walked back up here and I saw . . . you know that Buick? Well it was still sitting there. Shiny Red Car. And I'm looking in it checking it out and the fucking keys are only sitting there in the hole. So I thought toodle-oo, why not? You ever driven one Mickey?

MICKEY. What?

BABY. One of those big yank motors. Like sitting on a velvet cushion. Floating past Nelson's column, sitting on a velvet throne. Through Waterloo, down Camberwell, all the way, press a button, the roof comes off. Press another, the radio comes on. Cutlass on the back seat. I felt like General Patton.

And I parked it, right, and I asked around, and the first bloke I ask actually knows where Mr. Ross lives. Belly up, knock on the door. And this bloke with yellow hair answers. And I chopped him.

SKINNY. You did what?

BABY. Yeah. I chopped him on the top of the head with my dad's old sword. And he fell down. And he never got up again.

SWEETS. Baby, you chopped him. You chopped Mr. Ross?

BABY. Yeah. It's easier than you think. He just opens the door, and you chop him. (*Pause.*) So there's no-one around so I step inside. First door I try, the parlour, watching telly, sandwich on his knee, the one and only Silver Johnny. Bit surprised to see his old mate Baby in such a place, so I take him outside, walk him up and down, put him in the motor brung him back here. Except coming over Vauxhall the engine packs in. And the buses have all stopped so this one paid for a cab. (*Pause.*)

SKINNY. Baby? Did you kill him?

BABY. Well, Skinny Luke, I don't know. It's actually really difficult to tell . . .

POTTS. We're fucked. We're dead. I'm dead.

MICKEY, *who has heard all this, comes down the stairs.*

MICKEY. Sweets. Get upstairs.

SWEETS. Mickey –

MICKEY. Did you hear me. Do it now.

POTTS. Mickey what –

MICKEY. Fucking get up there. Do as I say. Get upstairs.

POTTS. We're going.

SKINNY. Mickey –

MICKEY. Do you want to die today? Eh? Do you want to die today.

POTTS. Oh my Sweet Life.

MICKEY. Do you want to die today. Get upstairs you fuck. Do as I say. Do as I say.

Exit SWEETS, POTTS *and* SKINNY, *upstairs. Very long pause.*

MICKEY. Are you all right?

BABY. Bearing up. (*Pause.*)

MICKEY. You spoken to him?

BABY. We did have a natter on the way. Yes.

MICKEY. Right. What did he say?

BABY. He told me.

MICKEY. Everything?

BABY. How's your head cold Mickey? You feeling alright?

MICKEY. What did he tell you?

BABY. Why don't we ask him. He's right there. He said when him and Dad left here and went to Ross's place, that when they got there, that you was there Mickey. He said that your head cold had miraculously disappeared. He said you was feeling better. He said you all played billiards. Did you play billiards Mickey?

MICKEY. Yes.

BABY. I see. He said that he was sent out the room to listen to some records. With this bloke with all tattoos. And then he said he came back an hour later, and you weren't there no more. And Dad weren't there no more. Isn't that right Johnny?

MICKEY. Baby, I had no choice. We were going to lose everything.

BABY. He's going a very odd shade. We probably ought to help him down.

MICKEY. Yes.

BABY. Help him down Mickey. Help Johnny down.

MICKEY *ungags* SILVER JOHNNY. *He lets out a note. A moan. Lost.*

BABY. It's all right John.

MICKEY *helps him down. He unties him.*

MICKEY. Are you all right?

SILVER JOHNNY. Fuck you. Fuck you Mickey.

SILVER JOHNNY *runs upstairs.*

BABY. Let him go. (*Pause.*) Fancy. You're sitting there with the telly on and your supper and all then all that. Eh? He was in remarkably good shape after. Even tipped the cab driver. That's the young eh? They really bounce back, don't they.

MICKEY. I'm going to talk now and tell me to shut up if I'm saying the wrong thing –

BABY. Shut up Mickey. Please. (*Pause.*) Will you tell me something Mickey? Were you actually in the room when they cut him in half?

Pause. MICKEY *shakes his head.*

You wasn't?

MICKEY. No.

BABY. Where was you?

MICKEY. I'd gone by then. I was back home.

BABY. Back home?

MICKEY. Yes. They said wait. (*Pause.*) They said if I went home I'd get . . . we'd get the club. We could keep the club.

BABY. *We?*

MICKEY. That I could keep the club.

BABY. Did you go to them? (*Pause.*)

MICKEY. Baby, this is a new time for both of us –

BABY. A new time. A new time. (*Pause.*) I like that Mickey. You have a very pleasant way with words.

MICKEY. Are you sure he's dead?

BABY. Who?

MICKEY. Mr. Ross. Because if he isn't . . .

BABY. Mickey, he's got his yellow hair parted right down between his eyes. And it's a hell of a schlep. And I think if he is coming he's going to need a jolly good lie down first.

MICKEY. Baby, I don't know what to do.

BABY (*copying*). Baby I don't know what to do.

MICKEY. I don't know what to do.

BABY. I don't know what to do.

MICKEY. *Baby I'm sorry.*

Pause. BABY *approaches* MICKEY.

BABY. Sometimes when I wake up I feel totally not there. I feel completely numb. And I think, Come on. Come alive. Feel it. Like you used to. But I'm numb. I lie there, and my mind spins on nothing. I hear people next door, in the next one along, fighting or laughing and I can't feel their . . . pain or nothing. (*Pause.*)

Woke up this afternoon, I just knew it was going to be one of those days. Beautiful, sunny, but one you're just not there for. Sorry Mickey. I just can't feel your pain.

Enter SWEETS *and* POTTS.

SWEETS. Mickey?

BABY. All right Sweets?

SWEETS. Mickey, we've got a problem.

BABY. What's that then?

SWEETS. Something's happened.

MICKEY (*quietly*). I'm dead. I'm dead.

BABY. What's the problem then?

SWEETS. Well, Silver Johnny said Mickey was round Mr. Ross's Saturday night.

MICKEY. I'm sorry.

POTTS. Mickey, what have you done? It was you. It was you, you cunt. This whole thing. Fucking head cold. You cunt.

SWEETS. It's not true is it Mickey? It's because he's been hanging upside down so long.

BABY. They're really rocking in Boston . . .

Enter SKINNY.

SKINNY. Relax. It's bullcrap. I know it's bullcrap.

SWEETS. I told you.

POTTS. How?

SKINNY. Little cunt's twiced us all wants to blame someone else. It's bullcrap.

SWEETS. What happened Mickey?

SKINNY. Mickey's done nothing. Bastard's been hanging upside down for two hours he's gone back to front. And I'll prove it. I'll prove it. Because Mickey was at home and then he came here. He was ill. He was ill then he came here. Anyone listens to some little fuck ditched us all in the lurch is a sissy. I believe Mickey. (*To* BABY.) Shut your fucking mouth, Jew. You don't belong here. You've got no place here. None of us want you. You're nasty and you lie. We've all had enough. Take your lies somewhere else.

BABY *walks across the room with the Derringer, puts it to* SKINNY*'s head and fires once.*

Oww. Fuck. Fuck. Fuck. What did you do that for?

Blood pours from the side of SKINNY*'s head.*

What did you do that for? What did you do that for?

POTTS. Skinny . . .

SWEETS. Skinny . . .

SKINNY. I'm shot in the head. I've been shot in the head . . .

POTTS. It's only the Derringer . . .

SWEETS. Help him.

POTTS. It's only the Derringer.

SKINNY. I've been shot in the head. Right in the fucking head.

POTTS. It's only the Derringer.

SKINNY. What do you mean it's only the Derringer? I'm shot. look at all this blood.

POTTS. Help him. Call a doctor.

SWEETS. We can't. We can't.

SKINNY. Call a doctor. I might die.

SWEETS. It's only the . . . it's only a little hole.

SKINNY. What did you do that for?

SWEETS. You'll be all right. You'll be all right.

SKINNY. I wasn't doing anything. I wasn't doing anything. I was only trying to help. You twat. You didn't have to . . . look. Look at all this blood. Look at all this fucking blood.

SWEETS. We've got to get a doctor.

MICKEY. Skinny sit down.

SWEETS. Sit down.

SKINNY. Look. I've got . . . I've fucked up my new trousers. I've got blood on my new trousers.

MICKEY. Try to relax. Get a towel.

SWEETS. Sid take your shirt off.

SKINNY. Fucking great. Fucking great. What if I die. What if I die eh? Did you think of that? What if I die. How much blood do you have to lose before you die?

POTTS. You've got to lose pints of the stuff. You'll be fine.

SKINNY. Look, I've lost, look. Mickey. That's about a pint right there. Have I got any on my back?

POTTS. Your back's fine. Your back's fine.

SKINNY. My teeth have all gone loose. Look. Feel. He's unshipped all my fucking teeth.

MICKEY. Sit down. You're all right.

SKINNY. Feel. My teeth have gone wiggly. How much blood have I lost.

POTTS. Hardly any. Sit down.

SKINNY. I've already lost at least two pints. How much do you have to lose Mickey. How much do you have to lose Mickey. Mickey? How much blood do you have to lose before that's it?

SKINNY *dies.* POTTS *has just taken his shirt off.*

POTTS. Skinny . . . (*Pause.*)

SWEETS. Is he all right? Skinny.

POTTS. I don't know.

SWEETS. Skinny. Sid, I think he's gone.

POTTS. Baby, I think he's gone.

MICKEY *falls to his knees to his knees next to* SKINNY*'s body.*

MICKEY. No. No. No! No! No! No!!!

SWEETS. Skinny? Skinny?

MICKEY. Skinny!!!

POTTS. Is he breathing.

MICKEY. No. No. No . . .

SWEETS. He might still be alive. Is he breathing?

POTTS. He's stopped.

SWEETS. He might still be . . .

SILVER JOHNNY *appears on the stairs.*

SWEETS. Skinny. For fuck's sake Skinny . . .

POTTS. Try to keep him warm.

SWEETS. I think he's gone. (*Pause.*)

MICKEY. No. No. No. No. No.

Pause.

I'm sorry. I'm sorry Luke. I'm sorry. I'm really really . . .

Pause. MICKEY *is hunched over* SKINNY's *body.* POTTS *stands above them. He kicks* MICKEY *in the stomach.*

POTTS. Let's get out of here.

SWEETS. Mickey. I thought you loved us. I thought you were my friend.

Exit SWEETS *and* POTTS. *Pause.* BABY *walks over to the desk and sits down.* SILVER JOHNNY *comes down the stairs.* MICKEY *lies on the floor, panting.* BABY *watches him.* SILVER JOHNNY *comes into the middle of the room. He watches* BABY.

BABY. Are you all right?

SILVER JOHNNY. Yes. Yes I am.

BABY. You sure? (*Pause.*) Are you dizzy?

SILVER JOHNNY. No. I'm fine.

BABY. That's good.

SILVER JOHNNY. I opened the windows.

BABY. I can smell the dawn. Good. Is the sun out?

SILVER JOHNNY. It's getting hot. Out in the street. There's people.

BABY. Good. Good. (*Pause.*) That's good. Do you want to go out there.

SILVER JOHNNY. What?

BABY. Out in the street. Get a nice cool drink. Walk around. It's lovely out this time. It's my favourite time of the day. Before anything happens.

SILVER JOHNNY. Okay.

BABY. Good. Good. Let's do that.

BABY *slips out of the Silver Jacket and leaves it on the floor. Exit* BABY *and* SILVER JOHNNY *into the light.* MICKEY *lies on the floor. Music.*

Curtain.

This revised edition of *Mojo* first published in Great Britain in 1996
as a paperback original by Nick Hern Books Limited, 14 Larden Road,
London W3 7ST in association with the Royal Court Theatre,
Sloane Square, London SW1W 8AS. First edition published in 1995
by Nick Hern Books.

Front cover image: Creative Hands

Typeset by Country Setting, Woodchurch, Kent TN26 3TB
Printed by Cox and Wyman Limited, Reading, Berks

ISBN 1 85459 366 8

A CIP catalogue record for this book is available from
the British Library